JOSEPH– GOD'S SUPERHERO

GENESIS 37-50

KAY ARTHUR
JANNA ARNDT

D1416405

HARVEST HOUSE PUBLISHERS
Eugene, Oregon 97402

All Scripture quotations are taken from the New American Standard Bible®, © 1960, 1962, 1963, 1968, 1971, 1972, 1973, 1975, 1977, 1995 by The Lockman Foundation. Used by permission.

Illustrations by Steve Bjorkman

Cover by Left Coast Design, Portland, Oregon

Discover 4 Yourself Bible Studies for Kids

JOSEPH—GOD'S SUPERHERO

Copyright © 2002 by Precept Ministries International
Published by Harvest House Publishers
Eugene, Oregon 97402

ISBN 0-7369-0739-4

Printed in the United States of America

02 03 04 05 06 07 08 09 / RDP-VS / 10 9 8 7 6 5 4 3 2 1

For my sons, Chase and Brent:

I am so blessed to see so much of Joseph in you—your integrity, your love, compassion, and forgiveness. May your knees always be bowed and your hearts surrendered to God. May you always have courage to do the right thing, enduring hardships with grace, knowing that a loving God holds you in His hands and will use all things for your good. May you give God all the glory. May you always be superheroes of the faith!

I love you with all my heart.
Mommy
Philippians 3:14

CONTENTS

Searching for Truth—
A Bible Study *You* Can Do!

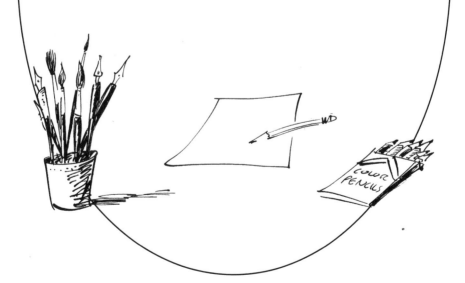

SEARCHING FOR TRUTH—
A BIBLE STUDY YOU CAN DO!

Hey! Look up here! Can you see us? Molly and I are in the tree house with Sam (the great detective beagle) planning our next adventure in God's Word. By the way, my name is Max. Guess where we're headed? New York City! My Aunt Sherry is developing a new comic book for Amazing Comics on the life of Joseph called *Joseph—God's Superhero.* Doesn't that sound exciting?

A hero is someone who is known for his acts of courage, who risks or sacrifices his life for other people. A comic-book superhero is someone like Superman, who can do the extraordinary like being faster than a speeding bullet and having X-ray vision.

WHAT makes Joseph God's superhero? Can he run faster than a speeding bullet like Superman? No! Unlike Superman, who is a fictional character with super powers, Joseph is a real person in the Bible who was just an ordinary guy like you and me.

So WHAT makes Joseph special? Does he do anything extraordinary? Is he courageous? WHAT is Joseph really like? You can find out by studying God's Word, the Bible, the source of all truth, and by asking God's Spirit to lead and guide you. You also have this book, which is an inductive Bible study. That word *inductive* means this study will help you investigate the life of Joseph in the Book of Genesis to discover *for yourself* what the Bible means, instead of depending on what someone else says it means.

So are you ready to head to New York City to learn how to make a comic book while you discover WHAT makes Joseph God's superhero? Great—then pack those bags! We'll see you at Amazing Comics!

THINGS YOU'LL NEED
▼

NEW AMERICAN STANDARD BIBLE
(UPDATED EDITION)—OR PREFERABLY,
THE NEW INDUCTIVE STUDY BIBLE
(NISB)
PEN OR PENCIL
COLORED PENCILS
INDEX CARDS
A DICTIONARY
THIS WORKBOOK

1

BETRAYAL AND THE PIT

GENESIS 37

How do you like New York City? Isn't it incredible? Everything is so big! Aunt Sherry is going to give us a tour of Amazing Comics, and then we can get to work discovering what God's Word has to say about a man named Joseph who lived almost 4000 years ago and yet is known today as a superhero.

Day One

DISCOVERING OUR SUPERHERO

"Are you ready for your first assignment?" asked Aunt Sherry as we sat around her desk and pulled out our notebooks. "WHAT should we do first before we begin our research on Joseph?"

Max smiled as he replied, "Pray!"

"That's right, Max. Bible study should always begin with prayer. We need God to direct us and teach us by His Spirit so that we can understand what He says in His Word. We need God to be our Master Editor to make sure we handle His Word accurately. So let's pray, and then you can begin your first assignment at Amazing Comics."

Your first assignment will be learning how to be a writer for a comic book by helping Aunt Sherry. Aunt Sherry is a writer. Not only does she think up story ideas to present to the editor, but she also has to think of story ideas that can be illustrated in an interesting way.

As Aunt Sherry writes and plans her story, she has to be able to think in pictures and use words to enhance those pictures. She tells the story by writing a script that looks a lot like a movie script. The script will tell how each page in the comic book should look, and it will also break down the pages into individual panels. Aunt Sherry also writes all the dialogue for the characters. When she is finished, the editor will read the script to check for any mistakes and make any needed changes.

So let's get started by helping Aunt Sherry develop our main character. Turn to the Observation Worksheets on page 119. Observation Worksheets are pages that have the Bible text printed out for you to use as you do your research on the life of Joseph.

Now read Genesis 37:1-4 and mark every reference to Joseph in a special way by coloring *Joseph* blue, along with any pronouns that also refer to Joseph. WHAT are pronouns? Check out Max and Molly's research notes below.

PRONOUNS

Pronouns are words that take the place of nouns. A noun is a person, place, or thing. A pronoun stands in for a noun! Here's an example: "Molly and Max are learning how to develop the characters in a comic book. They have to do lots of research." The word *they* is a pronoun because in the second sentence it takes the place of Molly's and Max's names. It is another word we use to refer to Molly and Max.

Watch for these other pronouns when you are marking people:

I	you	he	she	me	him	her
mine	yours	his	hers	we	it	our
its	they	them				

Now that you have marked *Joseph,* another thing writers do as they plan their script and research their characters is ask lots of questions. Asking questions helps them decide how to portray the characters in their story. Let's see WHAT we can learn about Joseph by asking the 5 W's and an H questions. What are the 5 W's and an H? They are the WHO, WHAT, WHERE, WHEN, WHY, and HOW questions.

1. Asking WHO helps you find out:

   WHO wrote this? To WHOM was it written?

   WHOM are we reading about? WHO said this or did that?

2. WHAT helps you understand:

   WHAT is the author talking about?

   WHAT are the main things that happen?

3. WHERE helps you learn:

   WHERE did something happen?

   WHERE did they go?

   WHERE was this said?

   When we discover a "where" we double-underline the "<u>where</u>" in green.

4. WHEN tells us about time. We mark it with a green clock like this:

   WHEN tells us:

   WHEN did this event happen or WHEN will it happen?

   WHEN did the main characters do something? It helps us to follow the order of events, which is so important to a writer.

5. WHY asks questions like:

   WHY did he say that? WHY did this happen?

   WHY did they go there?

6. HOW lets you figure out things like:

HOW is something to be done?

HOW did people know something had happened?

Let's do our research on Joseph by asking the 5 W's and an H. WHAT do these four verses in Genesis 37 on page 119 tell us about Joseph?

Genesis 37:1-2 WHO is Joseph's father?

_____

Genesis 37:1-2 WHERE is Joseph?

In the land of _____

Genesis 37:2 HOW old is Joseph?

_____

Genesis 37:2 WHOM is Joseph with?

_____

Genesis 37:2 WHAT is Joseph's job?

_____

Genesis 37:2 WHAT kind of report does Joseph bring to his father?

_____

Genesis 37:3 HOW does Israel feel about Joseph?

_____

WHY?_____

WHO is Israel? Did you know that Israel and Jacob are the same person? God changed Jacob's name to Israel in Genesis 35:9-10.

Genesis 37:3 WHAT did Israel make for Joseph?

_____

Genesis 37:4 HOW did Joseph's brothers feel about him?

_____

Genesis 37:4 WHY do you think they felt that way about Joseph?

_____

A SPECIAL COAT

Have you heard Bible stories about Joseph and his coat of many colors? The Bible calls it a *varicolored* tunic. WHAT was this varicolored tunic like? What made it special?

The Hebrew word that is used for varicolored in Genesis 37:3 is *pac*, or *pas*, which means "the palm of the hand or sole of the foot, a long and sleeved tunic."

Now in the time of history when Joseph lived, most workingmen wore short tunics that were sleeveless so they could keep their arms and legs free and make it easier for them to do their jobs.

Bible scholars think that this special tunic could have been a coat of leisure that showed Joseph's brothers that Joseph wasn't expected to work like they were, since work would have been very difficult in this full-length tunic.

By looking at Genesis 37, we see that this varicolored tunic showed Joseph's brothers that their father favored and loved Joseph the most, which caused their envy and hate.

Great research! Did you know that comic books often have a character profile page to help the reader learn important facts about the superhero featured in that comic book? Let's get a character profile started on Joseph, God's superhero. Look at the character profile below and fill in the facts that you have uncovered so far in your research. Don't try to answer all the facts—just the ones you have uncovered today.

CHARACTER PROFILE ON JOSEPH

Real name:

_____

Known as (called): the

_____

Also called a H __ __ __ e __

Occupations: _____

_____

Base of operations (where he lived):

_____

Where he moved: _____

Physical description: _____

_____

Superpowers (special abilities): _____

Source of superpowers: _____

Family: _____

_____

_____

Superhero character traits: _____

_____

_____

Mission: _____

We are off and running, but before we head to the subway, our editor, Miss Lil, has one more assignment for you—your memory verse for the week. We want you to be a superhero just like Joseph, and that means you need to know God's Word by hiding it in your heart. As part of your superhero training, you will be given a new memory verse each week.

But before you can get started learning this week's verse, it looks like Miss Lil needs help in the editing department. Some of the words in this week's verse are all mixed up. Be the editor and unscramble the mixed-up words in the parentheses. Then place the correct word in the blank beside the parentheses. After you have unscrambled the verse, write it on an index card and practice saying it aloud three times in a row, three times each day!

Now Israel (oveld) _____ Joseph (orme) _____ than all his (osns) _____, because he was the son of his old age; and he made him a (rivacorlode) _____ (utnic) _____. His (robthres) _____ saw that their (afther) _____ loved him more than all his brothers; and so they (ahetd) _____ him and could not (pseak) _____ to him on friendly terms.

—Genesis 37: 3-4

Great training—see you tomorrow!

DEVELOPING OUR CHARACTERS

"Wow! Look at that skyline, Max. These buildings are so tall!" Molly exclaimed as she looked out Aunt Sherry's office window.

"I know. I can't wait until Aunt Sherry takes us sightseeing," replied Max.

"How about I take you guys to a very different McDonald's for lunch today?" asked Aunt Sherry as she walked into her office.

"McDonald's?" questioned Max. "What's so different about McDonald's?"

"You'll see," replied Aunt Sherry. "But right now we better get back to work. Yesterday we discovered who Joseph's father was. We also found out that he had brothers who hated him. Today we need to continue to develop our characters. Let's do some more research on Joseph's family."

But first things first. What is the first thing you need to do? Pray! Spend some time with your Master Editor, God, and then you are ready to search for truth.

As we continue our research on Joseph's family, we need to put ourselves in context by reviewing the Book of Genesis. WHAT is context? Context is the setting in which something is found. This is very important in Bible study. Context is a combination of two words: *con,* which means "with," and *text,* which means "what is written." So when you look for context in the Bible, you look at the verses and chapters surrounding the passage you are studying, such as looking at the whole Book of Genesis, as well as seeing how it fits into the whole Bible.

Context also includes:

- The place something happens. (This is geographical context, such as knowing where Joseph lived. Did he live in the land of Canaan or in the United States?)

- The time in history an event happens. (This is historical context, such as, did Joseph live before Noah and the flood or after the flood?)

- The customs of a group of people. (This is cultural context. For instance, did Joseph wear a tunic or did he wear blue jeans?)

If you have already studied Genesis Part One *God's Amazing Creation* and Genesis Part Two *Digging Up the Past,* then you have discovered for yourself that the Book of Genesis is a book of generations. In Genesis 2:4 we see the generations of the heavens and the earth. In Genesis 5:1 we see the generations of Adam. We see Noah's generations in Genesis 6:9; Shem, Ham, and Japheth's generations in Genesis 10:1; Shem's generations in Genesis 11:10; and Terah's generations in Genesis 11:27. Now let's continue to look at the generations.

Look up and read Genesis 11:27. WHOM does Terah become the father of?

_____

Look up and read Genesis 21:1-3. WHOM did Abraham become the father of?

_____

Now read Genesis 25:19-26. WHOM did Isaac become the father of?

_____

And WHO did we discover was one of Jacob's sons?

_____

Good work! Now that we have Joseph's family background, let's take a closer look at Jacob, Joseph's father. Jacob was the son of Isaac and the grandson of Abraham. Jacob had a brother named Esau, and Jacob was called by two names: Jacob and Israel.

Let's find out HOW many sons Jacob had. Look up and read Genesis 35:22. HOW many sons did Jacob have?_____

Now read Genesis 35:22-29 and fill in the chart below of Jacob's sons by listing each son's name beside the name of his mother in order of his birth. Leah's name is listed on the chart twice because she gives birth to Jacob's first four sons, but her last two sons are numbers 9 and 10 in the birth order.

THE BIRTH ORDER OF JACOB'S SONS

Mother	Son
Leah	1. _____
	2. _____
	3. _____
	4. _____
Bilhah (Rachel's maid)	5. _____
	6. _____
Zilpah (Leah's maid)	7. _____
	8. _____
Leah	9. _____
	10. _____
Rachel	11. _____
	12. _____

Did you know that Jacob's two wives, Leah and Rachel, were sisters? Jacob married both of these sisters because his relative Laban (Leah and Rachel's father) tricked Jacob into marrying Leah when he thought he was marrying Rachel.

Look up and read Genesis 29:30-35.

Genesis 29:30 WHOM did Jacob love? _____

Genesis 29:31 WHY did God open Leah's womb and give her a son?

_____

Genesis 29:31. WHAT happens to Rachel?

_____

Barren means to not be able to have any children.
Read Genesis 30:22. WHAT happens to Rachel here?

_____

Read Genesis 35:16-19. WHAT happens to Rachel?

_____

Now go back and read Genesis 37:3-4 on your
Observation Worksheets on page 119. From all that we
have learned about Jacob, Leah, and Rachel, WHY do
you think Jacob loved Joseph more than all his sons?

_____

_____

WHY do you think Joseph's brothers hated him?

_____

_____

• Have you ever felt like your mom and dad loved
  your brother or sister or favored them more than you?
  _____ Yes _____ No

• WHAT did they do that made you feel that way?

_____

- HOW did you feel? Were you angry or hurt? Did you feel left out?

_____

_____

- Did it make you hate your brother or sister so that you could not even speak to them on friendly terms, like Joseph's brothers?

_____ Yes _____ No

If you answered yes to any of these questions, then keep your eyes open. You need to watch and see what happens to Joseph's brothers. Pay close attention to how they handle their feelings of hurt, anger, and jealousy. Do they allow their emotions to rule their behavior? We'll find out.

Now add Joseph's family to his character profile on page 12. You did a great job researching your character. Don't forget to work on your other assignment—your memory verse. Remember to practice it three times today, morning, noon, and night!

WRITING THE SCRIPT

"Here we are, guys: McDonald's, New York City style," laughed Aunt Sherry.

"This way, young ladies and gentleman," said the tuxedo-clad doorman as he opened the elegant glass door leading inside the neon-decorated McDonald's.

"Look at the flowers and candles on the marble tables, Max. Oh, and look—there's someone playing a piano!" exclaimed Molly as she spotted the maestro playing a Baldwin grand piano.

"What is he playing, Aunt Sherry?" asked Max.

"Chopin," replied Aunt Sherry.

"Chopin and hamburgers—I can't believe it!" replied Max. "And look at that! Isn't that one of those things that tells how the stock market is doing?"

"It sure is, Max. It is a digital ticker tape, and it announces the stock market prices because this McDonald's is located in Manhattan's financial district. Let's order, and when we're finished eating we'll go upstairs to the gift boutique to look for a souvenir."

"Cool—a store inside McDonald's! You're right, Aunt Sherry, we have never seen a McDonald's quite like this," laughed Max. "Let's go eat."

Now that we have had lunch, it's time to get back to work. Don't forget to pray and then head back to Genesis 37. Our background work is complete on Joseph and his family, so we need to start working on the script.

Let's turn to page 119 of our Observation Worksheets and start looking for key words. What are key words? Key words are words that pop up more than once. They are called key words because they help unlock the meaning of the chapter or book that you are studying and give you clues about what is most important in a passage of Scripture.

◎ Key words are usually used over and over again.

◎ Key words are important.

◎ Key words are used by the writer for a reason.

Once you discover a key word, you need to mark it in a special way using a special color or symbol so that you can immediately spot it in Scripture. Don't forget to mark any pronouns that go with the key words, too! Read Genesis 37 and mark the following key words.

tunic (draw a brown robe)

love (draw a red heart)

hate (draw a black heart with a jagged line through it)

dream (draw a blue cloud around it)

pit (draw a brown box around it and color it orange)

Don't forget to mark anything that tells you WHERE by double-underlining the <u>WHERE</u> in green. And don't forget to mark anything that tells you WHEN by drawing a green clock like this:

Your script is looking good! Tomorrow we will get to meet Amazing Comic's penciller as we begin to draw the first panels in our comic book. See you then!

SKETCHING THE PANELS

"Come on in, Max and Molly," called out Mr. Hetzel. "Are you ready to start creating the first panels in our comic book?"

"I can't wait," answered Molly. "I love to draw."

"Great. I also want you to meet our editor Miss Lil's son. This is Philip. Philip, this is Max, Miss Sherry's nephew, and this is Max's cousin Molly."

"Hi, Philip! Are you going to learn how to be a penciller, too?" asked Max.

"I sure am!" answered Philip. " I have been so excited that you and Molly were coming to visit. Mom said that I could help out with the comic book while you are here, and that we can also go with you and Miss Sherry as she shows you around New York City!"

"All right! That is so awesome," replied Max. "Can we bring Sam, too?"

"I think so, but we might have to sweet-talk Mom. She's heard all about Sam's adventures with your Uncle Jake," laughed Philip.

"Okay," laughed Max and Molly.

"Let's pray," said Mr. Hetzel, "and then we are ready to get to work."

Do you know what a penciller does? A penciller is the artist who draws the comic book in pencil. Every comic book needs a good penciller because the most important thing in a comic book is the drawings. The penciller takes the writer's ideas and turns them into real images on paper. The only way to become a good penciller is to draw, draw, draw. The more you practice, the better you will be. Pencillers keep a file, known as swipes. Swipes are photographs, drawings, etc., to help them learn how to draw certain objects. They also study other artists' work while they are learning to develop their own style.

Now each comic book page is broken down into different panels. A panel is a framed drawing that helps develop the story line. So, become the penciller. Grab your pencils, erasers, and swipes to get started as we draw the panels for Genesis 37.

Mr. Hetzel's Sketching Tips

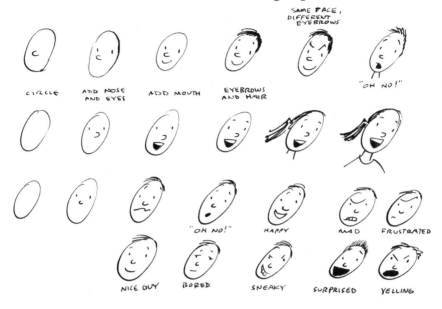

Turn to pages 119-120 of your Observation Worksheets. Read Genesis 37:5-11 and answer the 5W's and an H to help decide what to draw in your first panel.

WHO are the main characters?

_____

WHAT is the main thing that is happening?

_____

Genesis 37:7 WHAT was Joseph's first dream?

_____

Genesis 37:8 WHAT did the brothers think this dream meant?

_____

Genesis 37:9 WHAT was Joseph's second dream?

_____

Genesis 37:5,8,11 HOW do Joseph's brothers feel about him?

_____

Now sketch it out. Draw the first panel on page 28 to show the main thing in verses 5-11.

Read Genesis 37:12-17.
Genesis 37:13-14 WHAT does Israel do?

_____

Genesis 37:14-17 WHAT does Joseph do?

_____

Turn to page 28 and draw this second panel.

Read Genesis 37:18-24.
Genesis 37:18 WHAT do the brothers do when they see Joseph coming?

_____

Genesis 37:19 WHAT do they call Joseph?

_____

(Add this description to Joseph's character profile under "Known as" on page 12.)

Genesis 37:21 WHO doesn't want to kill Joseph? And which son is he in the birth order (page 16)?

_____

Genesis 37:22 WHAT is this brother's suggestion?

_____

WHY? WHAT was he going to do later?

_____

Genesis 37:23-24 WHAT do the brothers do?

_____

Now before you draw your third panel, take a look at Genesis 42:21.

Genesis 42:21 HOW did Joseph feel when he was thrown into the pit? WHAT did the brothers see?

_____

WHAT did Joseph do?

_____

Draw the third panel on page 28 to show what happens in Genesis 37:18-24.

How could Joseph's brothers be so mean? Have you ever called your brother or sister names?
_____ Yes   _____ No

WHAT names did you call them?

_____

WHY?_____

_____

Have you ever been jealous of your brother or sister?
____ Yes   ____ No

WHY?_____

_____

Did you notice how they stripped Joseph of the tunic that showed that he was special to their father? Have they allowed jealousy, hurt, and anger to take over? Yes—otherwise how could they plot to kill their own brother?

Can you imagine how hot and thirsty Joseph must have felt being thrown into a pit with no water? Do you think he was scared and confused?
____ Yes   ____ No

How would you feel if you were treated like Joseph?

_____

Have you ever treated your brother or sister badly?
____ Yes   ____ No

If you have, what should you do? Should you ask your brother or sister to forgive you? ____ Yes   ____ No

WHY?_____

_____

We'll find out what Joseph does as we continue our search to find out what made Joseph God's superhero.

PENCILING IT IN

Hey, guys, it's back to the drawing board. We have a lot more to learn as we continue to pencil Genesis 37. Mr. Hetzel is giving Max, Molly, and Philip a few more tips on becoming a good penciller.

"Remember, it is very important to make sure your characters always look consistent," said Mr. Hetzel as he examined the kids' sketches. "The characters should look the same in each panel. If a character has long hair in one panel, he shouldn't have short hair in the next. Also remember to leave space in your drawings so the letterer will have room to add the characters' dialogue. Your sketches are getting better and better. Keep up the good work."

Let's get ready to sketch. Don't forget to pray and then turn to page 121 and read Genesis 37:25-28.

WHAT do the brothers do with Joseph?

_____

Turn to page 28 and draw the fourth panel.

Read Genesis 37:29-36.
Genesis 37:29 WHAT did Reuben find when he returned?

_____

Was Reuben there when Joseph was sold?

_____

Genesis 37:31-32 WHAT did the brothers do?

_____

Genesis 37:33-34 WHAT did Jacob do?

_____

Genesis 37:34-35 HOW did Jacob feel?

_____

Can you believe the brothers would lie to their father and let him think his favorite son was dead? How could they be so mean and cruel to their own father? Genesis 37:36 WHAT happened to Joseph?

_____

Draw the last panel on page 28.

What do you think it felt like to be a 17-year-old boy who was kidnapped, taken to a foreign country, and sold as a slave by his own brothers? How would you feel: scared, lonely, and rejected, or angry and determined to get even?

_____

We'll find out how Joseph handles his feelings as we continue our study in God's Word. Now before you head out with Max, Molly, Sam, and Philip for a little weekend fun, don't forget to say your memory verse to a grown-up. Flex those superhero muscles!

Genesis 37:5-11

Genesis 37:12-17

Genesis 37:18-24

Genesis 37:25-28

Genesis 37:29-36

2

FROM A DUNGEON TO THE PALACE

GENESIS 39-41

"New York City is made up of five boroughs, called the Bronx, Brooklyn, Manhattan, Queens, and Staten Island," Philip stated as he, Max, Molly, and Sam walked down the streets of New York along with his mom, Miss Lil, and Aunt Sherry on their first sight-seeing tour.

"What are we going to do first?" asked Max.

"How about a trip to the Metropolitan Museum of Art?" Aunt Sherry asked. "It is one of the greatest museums in the world. It has a wonderful collection of Egyptian art, and now that we know Joseph has been sold as a slave to Egypt, we can find out what Egypt was like."

"That's a great idea," replied Molly. "Let's go!"

LEARNING TO LETTER

"Look at that, Molly," Max said as he headed toward the Temple of Dendur. "There are so many awesome exhibits here. I really like 'The Met'!"

"Me, too," replied Molly. "I can't wait to learn how to re-create some of these awesome pieces of Egyptian jewelry with this bead kit."

"Well, while you're re-creating Egyptian jewelry, Philip and I are going to learn the ancient technique of reverse painting," Max replied.

How about you? Did you like "The Met"?

Now that we have experienced a little of ancient Egypt by visiting the museum, let's find out what is happening with our superhero.

Turn to page 124. Read Genesis 39 and mark the following key words and key phrase on your Observation Worksheet. WHAT is a key phrase? A *key phrase* is like a key word, except it is a group of words that are repeated instead of just one word, such as the phrase "I did it, I did it, I did it." The group of words *I did it* is a key phrase because it is a group of words that are repeated, instead of just one word. Don't forget to mark any pronouns that go with those key words or the key phrase. Also mark everything that tells you WHERE by double-underlining the <u>WHERE</u> in green. Mark everything that tells you WHEN with a green clock like this: 🕐

And the Lord was with Joseph (This is a key phrase. Draw a purple circle around it.)

God (Lord) (draw a purple triangle and color it yellow)

blessed (draw a blue cloud and color it pink)

sin (color it brown) (Even though sin is only mentioned once, it is a key word because knowing about sin is very important.)

Hebrew (draw a blue Star of David)

Now that you have marked your script, let's head over to Marie's office to learn how to be a letterer for our comic book. The letterer hand prints all of the dialogue, captions, and words in the comic book, and also places the word balloons where they need to go in each panel. Word balloons look like this: ( ) Most letterers will use a pencil first and then go over the letters in ink and erase the pencil marks.

So grab those pencils and erasers and let's practice. Before you can begin to letter, you have to know where you want to place your letters and how large you need to write. We have used an Ames lettering guide (it's like a ruler) to draw the guidelines printed out in the circle on the next page. Marie has lettered some of the words from your memory verse inside the circle. Find your verse by reading Genesis 39:19-23. Which one of these verses contains the words printed inside the circle? To practice lettering, take a pencil and print your memory verse using the guidelines inside the circle. Once you have finished lettering, practice saying this verse aloud how many times in a row? And how many times today? All right! What a superhero! You have an amazing memory!!

But _____
Lord _____
Joseph _____
kindness _____
and _____
in _____
the _____
Genesis 39: _____

_____

SETTING THE SCENE

You are doing fantastic at learning all the different jobs that make up a comic book. Today we are going to head back to Aunt Sherry's office to work on our script. We need to answer the 5W's and an H. Grab those scripts you marked yesterday.

Let's get started by doing WHAT first? P __ __ __ __ __ __. Good job! Your Master Editor is sooooooo proud of you! Now let's read Genesis 39 on pages 124-126.

Genesis 39:1 WHERE was Joseph taken?

_____

Genesis 39:1 WHO bought Joseph?

_____

Genesis 39:2 Was Joseph abandoned? WHO was with Joseph?

_____

Genesis 39:2 WHAT did Joseph become?

A _____ man.

Genesis 39:3-4 HOW did Joseph become prosperous?

_____

Genesis 39:4-6 WHAT was Joseph's relationship to his master, the Egyptian?

_____

Genesis 39:5 HOW did the Lord treat the Egyptian?

_____

Genesis 39:6 WHAT did Joseph look like?

_____

Genesis 39:7 WHO tempted Joseph?

_____

Genesis 39:7 WHAT did she ask Joseph to do?

_____

Genesis 39:8-9 HOW did Joseph respond?

_____

WHAT did Joseph say? "HOW then could I_____

_____?"

Genesis 39:10 Did Potiphar's wife accept Joseph's answer and leave him alone?

_____

Genesis 39:12 WHAT did Joseph do?

_____

Now let's do some cross-referencing. WHAT is cross-referencing? Cross-referencing is where we compare Scripture with Scripture by going to other passages in the Bible. This is a very important Bible study tool that we can use as we search out the meaning of Scripture because we know that Scripture never contradicts Scripture.

Look up 1 Corinthians 6:18. WHAT are we to do?

_____

Is that what Joseph did? ____ Yes ____ No

Yes! Joseph knew that it was immorality (a sin) to lie with someone who not only wasn't his wife but was also someone else's wife. Joseph was a young, handsome man, and even though he may have been tempted to sin, he did not. He fled, leaving WHAT behind?

_____

Joseph didn't wait. He didn't hesitate. He chose to honor God. He fled from sin. Joseph knew to WHOM his body belonged. HOW about you? Look up 1 Corinthians 6:19-20. WHAT is your body?

_____

Do you belong to yourself? _____ Yes _____ No

WHY or why not?

_____

_____

Did you know that you were bought with a price? Jesus died on a cross to pay the price for our sins.

> *He made Him who knew no sin to be sin on our behalf, so that we might become the righteousness of God in Him (2 Corinthians 5:21).*

1 Corinthians 6:20 WHOM are you to glorify?

_____

Now that we have seen our superhero in action, fleeing a difficult situation, let's see what happens next.

Genesis 39:13-19 WHAT did Potiphar's wife do?

_____

_____

Did she lie about Joseph?

_____

Genesis 39:20 WHAT happened to Joseph?

_____

HOW would you feel if you were put in jail for something you didn't do? Joseph was innocent. Potiphar's wife lied.

Have you ever gotten in trouble for something you didn't do? ____ Yes   ____ No

Did it make you mad? Did you cry, "It's not fair"? HOW did you respond?

_____

_____

Even though Joseph was innocent, God still let him go to jail. Did God abandon Joseph? Look at Genesis 39:21. WHERE is God and WHAT does He do?

_____

Genesis 39:22-23 HOW does the chief jailer treat Joseph?

_____

Genesis 39:23 WHAT happens to everything Joseph does?

_____

WHY?

_____

Isn't that awesome? Even though Joseph is in jail, we see that he is not alone. God has not forsaken him. He is right there with Joseph, extending His kindness to him, training him to be His superhero. Wow!

UNMASKING OUR SUPERHERO

As our story unfolds, we are beginning to see what it takes to be God's superhero. Being a superhero takes developing a strong and godly character, and the training isn't easy. Look at all Joseph has been through as God shapes and molds him to be His superhero. He goes from favorite son and hated brother to being kidnapped, sold as a slave, and thrown in jail. HOW would you handle these circumstances? Do you have the right stuff to be a superhero for God? Let's find out. Take a look at the character traits that God is developing in Joseph. Do you have these character traits?

CHARACTER TRAIT #1: FAITH

Faith is believing God; it is taking Him at His Word. It is when you believe what God says in the Bible, and it shows by the way you act. You decide to do what God wants you to do. Joseph's actions showed that he trusted and believed God.

Do you have faith?

- Have you placed your trust in Jesus Christ?
  ____ Yes   ____ No

- Do you believe what God says in His Word?
  ____ Yes   ____ No

- Do your actions show that you believe?
  ____ Yes   ____ No

Develop those faith muscles by studying God's Word and praying every day.

CHARACTER TRAIT #2: INTEGRITY

Integrity is being trustworthy and sincere. A person with integrity has the highest standards. It is being honest, pure, and consistent. Integrity is living by God's standards. Having the quality of integrity is doing the right thing when no one else is looking.

Joseph was trustworthy and sincere. He kept himself pure by fleeing temptation. He did the right thing. He followed God's standards.

Do you have integrity?

- Are you honest and trustworthy? Do you lie to your parents, cheat at school, or steal? ____ Yes   ____ No

- If your parents give you money to buy something, do you keep the change without asking? ____ Yes   ____ No

- Are you keeping yourself pure? Are you careful about the things you watch on TV and look at on the Internet? ____ Yes   ____ No

- WHAT kind of books and magazines do you read?

- If a friend tells a dirty joke, do you speak up, or do you laugh like everyone else?

_____

CHARACTER TRAIT #3: COURAGE

Courage is bravery and fearlessness. It is boldness, taking a stand, and doing what you know is right, even though you are afraid. It is also being able to admit when you are wrong. Joseph had courage. He was brave even though he was taken from his home, sold as a slave, and thrown in jail. Joseph was bold—he was able to tell his master's wife no.

Are you courageous?

- If your friends ask you to go to a party and you know they will be drinking, would you take a stand and say no? ____ Yes ____ No

- WHAT do you do if kids ask you to do something that is wrong, something you know you shouldn't do?

_____

- If you make a mistake, do you admit it? Can you say, "I'm sorry. I was wrong"? ____ Yes ____ No

CHARACTER TRAIT #4: SELF-DISCIPLINE

Self-discipline is learning to train and control your behavior. It is being able to turn away from temptation. It is choosing to do what is right, even when it is hard and difficult. Self-discipline is when you are able to stick to something even though it may be dull and boring. It requires determination and sacrifice. Joseph was self-disciplined. He chose to do the right thing. He worked hard for his master, he fled from temptation, and he worked hard in jail. He did not let his emotions rule.

Do you have self-discipline?

- Do you know how to control your temper and your tongue? _____ Yes _____ No

- Do you know how to wait for something that you want (or do you have to have it right now)? _____ Yes _____ No

Develop your self-discipline muscles.

- Do something difficult every day.

- Learn how to play a musical instrument or how to play a sport. Practice every day, and don't give up or quit, even when it gets hard or boring.

- Keep memorizing God's Word.

- Save your money for something special, instead of asking Mom and Dad to buy it for you.

- Surprise your parents. Do your homework every day without your parents reminding you and without complaining.

- Keep your room clean without being asked.

The training is hard, but you are on your way to becoming God's superhero. Now go back to page 12 and record all that you learned today about Joseph on his profile, including his superhero character traits.

CREATING THE DIALOGUE

"Hey, guys, come on in," Marie called out as she spotted Max, Molly, Philip, and Sam in her office doorway. "Today I am going to show you how to do the word balloons for a comic book. But first we need to check our script to get all the facts before we start lettering. So let's pray, and then we are ready to go."

Turn to your Observation Worksheets on page 126 and read Genesis 40. You need to mark the following key words:

God (draw a purple triangle and color it yellow)

dream (put a blue cloud around it)

Hebrew (draw a blue Star of David)

Now that we have marked our script, we need to ask the 5 W's and an H.

Genesis 40:1-2 WHO offends the king of Egypt?

_____

Genesis 40:3 WHAT happens to them?

_____

Genesis 40:4 WHO is in charge of these two prisoners?

_____

Genesis 40:5 WHAT happens to these two men on the same night?

_____

Genesis 40:6-8 HOW did they feel the next morning?

_____

WHY?_____

Genesis 40:7-8 WHAT does Joseph do?

_____

_____

Genesis 40:9-11 WHAT is the cupbearer's dream?

_____

_____

_____

Genesis 40:12-13 WHAT is the meaning of this dream?

_____

Genesis 40:14-15 WHAT did Joseph ask the cupbearer to do for him?

_____

Genesis 40:16-17 WHAT is the chief baker's dream?

_____

_____

_____

Genesis 40:18-19 WHAT is the meaning of this dream?

_____

Genesis 40:20-22 WHAT day is it?

_____

WHAT happened to the cupbearer?

_____

WHAT happened to the chief baker?

_____

Genesis 40:23 WHAT did the cupbearer do?

_____

Now that we have the facts, let's work on the dialogue for our word balloons that are drawn in the five panels on the next page. Word balloons tell the readers what the characters are thinking and saying. The letterer uses different types of word balloons to show if the character is thinking to himself, yelling, or whispering. Check out how these different word balloons are used by looking at Marie's sketch pad.

Now practice being the letterer by looking at the five panels drawn from Genesis 40 on the next page. Make up the dialogue for each character's word balloons by looking at your script.

You did a terrific job creating and lettering the dialogue! Now before you put what you learned about Joseph on his character profile, notice what our superhero is doing in Genesis 40:3-8. Our superhero is not sitting around angry, bitter, or feeling sorry for himself. Instead we see that not only is he in charge of these prisoners, but he is also reaching out and asking these two prisoners why they are sad. Another superhero character trait is revealed:

CHARACTER TRAIT #5: COMPASSION

Compassion is caring for those in need. Despite all that Joseph has been through, he shows caring and concern for his two fellow prisoners.

Do you have a heart of compassion? Do you reach out to those who are in need? ____ Yes   ____ No

Be a superhero—show compassion by:

- Visiting a nursing home

- Making a card for someone who is lonely or hurting

- Noticing when a friend is sad or angry and asking him how you can help

- Being a friend to someone who has been left out, inviting him to come over to your house

Now add all that you learned about Joseph in Genesis 40 to his profile on page 12. And don't forget to practice your memory verse!

BREAKING DOWN THE SCRIPT

Max looked up as Mr. Hetzel walked into Aunt Sherry's office carrying Sam. "Are you missing someone, Max?"

"Oh no! Where did you find him?" Max asked.

"He was a few doors down in the conference room, munching on the bagels and cream cheese."

"Sam, how could you? Now you're going to have to sit in your doggie cage until lunchtime. Bad, bad dog! Sorry, Mr. Hetzel. He's been so good that we took him off his leash. I should have noticed he was missing."

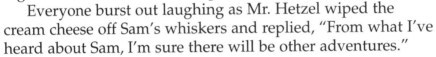

"It's okay, Max. No harm done, and everyone got quite a laugh out of it. You should have seen him standing halfway in the chair and halfway on the table licking the cream cheese."

"Oh, I can't believe I missed seeing Sam in action," cried Philip.

Everyone burst out laughing as Mr. Hetzel wiped the cream cheese off Sam's whiskers and replied, "From what I've heard about Sam, I'm sure there will be other adventures."

"I hope not," laughed Aunt Sherry. "Come on. Let's go see if they need any help cleaning up the conference room, and then we need to get back to work."

Now that Sam's adventure is over, you need to mark the following key words on your script, along with any pronouns or synonyms that go with them. WHAT are synonyms? Check out Max and Molly's research below.

SYNONYMS

Synonyms are different words that mean the same thing.
For example, *sailboat, yacht,* and *rowboat* are different words, but they are all names of types of boats. That's a synonym.

Now turn to your Observation Worksheets on page 128. Read Genesis 41 and mark the following key words:

God (draw a purple triangle and color it yellow)

dream (put a blue cloud around it)

Hebrew (draw a blue Star of David)

interpret (interpretation, explain) (color it pink)

famine (box it in black and color it brown)

abundance (plenty) (color it yellow)

Also mark everything that tells you WHERE by double-underlining the WHERE in green. Mark everything that tells you WHEN with a green clock like this:
Now answer the 5 W's and an H.

Genesis 41:2-4 WHAT is Pharaoh's first dream about?

Seven _____ that are sleek and fat are eaten by seven ugly and gaunt cows.

Genesis 41:5-7 WHAT is Pharaoh's second dream about?

Seven _____ that are plump and good are swallowed by seven ears that were thin and scorched by the east wind.

Genesis 41:8 WHAT did Pharaoh do in the morning?

Pharaoh called for all the _____ of Egypt and all its wise men and told them his dreams, but there was no one who could interpret them.

Genesis 41:9-13 WHO tells Pharaoh about Joseph?

The chief _____

Genesis 41:1 HOW long has it been since the cupbearer was released from prison in Genesis 40:23 until Pharaoh's dream in Genesis 41:1?

_____

Wow, Joseph sure has been waiting a long time!

Genesis 41:14-15 WHY does Pharaoh bring Joseph out of the dungeon? To _____ his dream.

Genesis 41:16 HOW does Joseph respond to Pharaoh?

"It is not in me; _____ will give Pharaoh a favorable answer."

Genesis 41:28-31 WHAT did Pharaoh's dream mean?

There will be seven years of great _____

in the land of Egypt, and after them seven years of

_____ will ravage the land.

Genesis 41:33 WHAT did Joseph tell Pharaoh to do?

"Let Pharaoh look for a man discerning and wise, and

_____ him over the land of Egypt."

Genesis 41:34-36 WHAT actions did Joseph tell Pharaoh to take?

Appoint _____ in charge of the land.

Gather and _____ up the grain for food.

Let them _____ it.

Genesis 41:37-41 WHOM did Pharaoh choose to be over

the land of Egypt? _____

Genesis 41:39 HOW does Pharaoh describe Joseph in
this verses?

discerning and _____

Genesis 41:39-40 WHO is the only person greater than
Joseph?

_____

Genesis 41:42-45 WHAT does Pharaoh give Joseph?

Pharaoh took off his signet _____, clothed him in

garments of fine _____, put the gold

_____ around his neck, had him ride in

his second _____, and gave him

_____ as his wife.

Genesis 41:46 HOW old is Joseph when he stands before

Pharaoh? _____ old

Genesis 41:47-49 WHAT did Joseph do during the seven
years of plenty? He stored up _____ in
great abundance like the sand of the sea. It was beyond
measure.

Genesis 41:50-52 WHAT happens to Joseph before the

year of famine? Joseph has two _____.

WHAT are their names? _____ and

_____

Genesis 41:56-57 WHAT did Joseph do during the famine?

Joseph opened all the _____ and sold grain to the Egyptians and to the people of all the earth.

Now be creative. Find the words from each blank in the word search below.

S	C	C	E	S	I	W	T	S	O	N	S	W	E
N	U	H	O	A	R	A	H	P	I	T	E	S	N
A	P	A	N	W	H	T	I	A	U	S	×	R	I
I	ß	R	I	N	T	E	R	P	R	E	T	E	M
C	E	I	A	R	E	G	T	S	T	O	R	E	A
I	A	O	R	Z	F	E	Y	N	Y	A	I	S	F
G	R	T	G	O	A	H	Y	Y	q	ß	S	R	W
A	E	N	S	T	O	R	E	H	O	U	S	E	S
M	R	R	A	S	E	N	A	T	H	N	N	V	W
Z	A	G	U	A	R	D	R	q	M	D	E	O	O
E	M	M	A	N	A	S	S	E	H	A	N	R	C
T	W	O	Y	E	A	R	S	E	Z	N	I	I	D
E	C	A	L	K	C	E	N	S	A	C	L	N	O
M	I	A	R	H	P	E	S	O	J	E	E	G	G

Wow! Did you notice that our superhero was 30 years old when he stood before Pharaoh? It has been 13 years since Joseph was kidnapped, sold as a slave, and put in a jail. WHAT superhero character trait does this reveal?

CHARACTER TRAIT #6: ENDURANCE

Endurance is being able to withstand hardship or stress. It means to persevere, to not give up. Joseph is a picture of endurance. His life was full of hardship, but he never complained, he kept going, and he never gave up. Develop this character trait of endurance:

- Try climbing a rock-climbing wall. Don't give up until you reach the top.

- Work on a difficult jigsaw puzzle until it is complete.

- Run a little every day until you are able to run a mile.

- Go to the library and pick out a classic book and read it.

WHAT other trait does God's superhero reveal as Pharaoh brings him out of the dungeon?

CHARACTER TRAIT #7: HUMILITY

Humility is a lack of pride. It is submission. Humility is knowing our weaknesses as well as our strengths. It is recognizing God as the Giver of all gifts. Joseph was humble. He told Pharaoh, "I don't have the answers, but God does." Joseph also acknowledged God for his fruitfulness. When Pharaoh asks where he can find someone to be in charge of the land of Egypt, Joseph doesn't say, "Hey, Pharaoh, I'm right here. Put me in charge of the land of Egypt. After all, I told you what the dreams meant!" Instead, he waited. He submitted to God's will.

Are you humble?

- Do you thank God for your talents and the things you have? ____ Yes ____ No

- Do you brag about your accomplishments, or do you give God the credit?

_____

Turn to page 12, and add all that you learned about Joseph to his superhero profile.

Now that Joseph is released from prison and put in charge of the land of Egypt, we see that only Pharaoh has a position higher than his. Do you see how God has been using Joseph's circumstances to mold and make him into a leader, to prepare him for what was to come? As we continue to develop our comic book, watch our superhero in action to see how God uses all things—including the hard, difficult, and bad things—for good.

Day Five
LAYING IT OUT

Yesterday we were amazed as we watched Pharaoh bring Joseph out of the dungeon to interpret his dream and then set him over the land of Egypt, giving him gifts, a wife, and pro-claiming that the Egyptians should bow before him. All of a sudden, Joseph goes from being a slave to being a ruler, and from living in a dungeon to living in a palace. Isn't that incredible? As we have worked on our script, we have been marking every reference to *God* and *Lord* on our Observation Worksheets. Today let's go back to Genesis 39–41 on pages 124-133 and look for every place that you marked *God* and *Lord*. Make a list of everything you learn about God.

GOD

Genesis 39:2 The Lord _____ _____ Joseph.

Genesis 39:3 The Lord _____ all that Joseph
      did to _____.

Genesis 39:5 The Lord _____ the Egyptian's
      house on account of Joseph.

      The Lord's _____ was upon
      _____ that he (the Egyptian) owned, in the
      house and in the field.

Genesis 39:21 The Lord _____ _____ Joseph
      and _____ _____ to
      him, and _____ him _____ in
      the sight of the chief jailer.

Genesis 39:23 The Lord _____ _____ Joseph and
      whatever he did the Lord _____ to
      _____.

Genesis 40:8 _____ belong to God.

Genesis 41:16 God _____ _____ Pharaoh a
      favorable answer.

Genesis 41:28 God _____ _____ to Pharaoh
      what He is _____ _____ _____.

Genesis 41:32 The matter is _____ by God.

      God _____ quickly _____ it _____.

Genesis 41:39 God has _____ you.

Genesis 41:51 God has _____ me _____

all my trouble and all my father's household.

Genesis 41:52 God has _____ me _____ in

the land of my _____.

Wow! WHAT does this list show us about the character of
God?

GOD IS SOVEREIGN

Look up and read Isaiah 46:8-11.

Is there anyone like God? ____ Yes   ____ No

WHAT will God accomplish? _____

Does God do what He says? ____ Yes   ____ No

God is the One in control. That means He is sovereign.
God is the Ruler of all. What He says, He will do. What He
plans will come to pass. God is over the entire earth. God was
in control of Joseph's circumstances, both good and bad. God
had a plan for Joseph's life. As you look up these scriptures in
your Bible, you may want to write in the margin what the
verse shows you about God (such as writing "God is
sovereign" beside Isaiah 46:8-11).

GOD IS OMNISCIENT

Look up and read Psalm 139:1-6.

Psalm 139:4 WHAT does God know?

_____

God knows everything: past, present, or future. God is
omniscient. That means He is all-knowing. He gave the
dreams and the interpretations of the dreams. Only God has
the answers and knows the future. God knew that He was
going to send a famine, so God trained and placed Joseph in a
place of leadership to prepare for the coming famine.

GOD IS OMNIPOTENT

Look up and read Job 42:2.

WHAT did Job know about the Lord?

God can _____ _____ _____.

No _____ of God's can be _____.

Omnipotent means that God is all-powerful. He had a purpose for the things He allowed to happen to Joseph. God rescued Joseph from his brothers who hated him so much that they wanted to kill him. God sent the seven years of abundance, as well as the famine.

GOD IS OMNIPRESENT

Look up and read Jeremiah 23:23-24. WHERE is God?

_____

Does God see everything? _____ Yes   _____ No

WHAT does God fill?

_____

Omnipresent means that God is present everywhere, at all times. God was with Joseph in the land of Canaan, in Egypt, in Potiphar's house, and in the king's prison. God is always near.

GOD IS IMMUTABLE

Look up and read Malachi 3:6.

WHAT do you see about the Lord?

_____

God is always the same in His nature, His character, and His will. He never changes. That means He is immutable. He is the same yesterday, today, and tomorrow. Joseph could trust God no matter what his circumstances were because he knew God's character; he knew that God had not changed.

God is Gracious and Merciful

Look up and read Psalm 145:8-9.

WHAT do you see about the Lord?

The Lord is _____ and _____.

The Lord is slow to _____ and great in

_____.

The Lord is _____ to _____.

The Lord's _____ are over all His works.

God is gracious and merciful. He blessed Potiphar and his house on account of Joseph. God extended His kindness to Joseph in prison. God is good. He made Joseph forget all his trouble and made him fruitful.

God is Faithful

Look up and read Deuteronomy 7:9.

WHAT kind of God is He? _____

WHAT does God keep? _____

_____

God is always true to His promises. How many times in your list did you see that God was with Joseph? _____ times. Isn't that awesome? God was faithful. He was always there.

God is Eternal

Look up and read Revelation 1:8.

WHAT is God? The _____ and

_____, who _____, who _____;

and who _____ _____ _____. God is the

_____.

God is eternal. That means He has no beginning or end. He is not confined to time. All of Joseph's circumstances happened in God's perfect timing. God brought Joseph to Egypt, He trained and prepared Joseph, God put the cupbearer in prison with Joseph, God gave Pharaoh the dreams, and God caused the cupbearer to remember Joseph all in His timing.

Now that you have seen God's character, you can understand why Joseph was able to endure his circumstances, why he was able to wait patiently, and why he never grew angry or bitter. Joseph knew God. He understood God's character.

Do you know God? Do you have a relationship with Him like Joseph did? Why don't you spend some time thanking God for all you have learned about Him? Tell Him that you know He alone is God and that you will turn your life over to Him and allow Him to do whatever He pleases in your life, just like Joseph did. Tell God you want to please Him. Allow God to train you to be His superhero, no matter what the cost.

Now say your memory verse to a friend or a grown-up. Then watch out New York City—here we come!

3
FAMINE AND FAMILY

GENESIS 42-47

"Wow! Just look! That is so awesome," exclaimed Max as he looked out over New York's harbor from the window in the crown of the Statue of Liberty.

"Did you know that the Statue of Liberty was given to the American people as a gift of friendship from France?" asked Philip as he looked out the window, too.

"Why?" Molly asked.

"Well, because France admired the United States' struggle for freedom. Did you notice the chains at her feet? Those chains represent the United States' courage when its people overcame slavery. 'Lady Liberty' is crushing the chains of slavery."

"I didn't know that," replied Molly as they left the windows and headed back down the stairs inside the Statue of Liberty. "This is so much fun!"

"It sure is," agreed Max. "Thanks, Aunt Sherry."

"You're welcome," Aunt Sherry replied. "Now let's head back to the boat. We have a lot more to see."

ADDING THE DETAILS

That was a great trip! We hope you had as much fun as we did checking out New York City and "Lady Liberty." As we get back to work today creating our comic book, we need to turn to our Observation Worksheets on page 132. Don't forget to spend some time with your Master Editor. Then grab your script and put yourself in context. Read Genesis 41:50-57.

Genesis 41:50 WHEN did Joseph have his sons?

Before the _____ of _____

Genesis 41:51 WHY did Joseph name the firstborn Manasseh?

_____

Genesis 41:52 WHY did Joseph name the second son Ephraim?

_____

Genesis 41:54 WHAT has just begun in all the lands?

_____

At the beginning of the seven years of abundance, when Pharaoh set Joseph over the land of Egypt, Joseph is 30 years old. HOW old would Joseph be as the famine begins in Genesis 41:53-57?

_____

We have also seen that God is omnipotent (all-powerful), which means He could have prevented the famine. So WHY would an all-powerful and sovereign God allow the famine to happen? Let's find out by looking at some other passages of Scripture to see what they tell us about famines. Look up the following scriptures and answer the 5W's and an H to complete the crossword puzzle on famine.

Read Psalm 105:16-22.

1. (Across) WHO sent the famine? WHO is this "He"? (If you don't know, look back at verse 7.) _____

Read Jeremiah 29:17-19.

2. (Down) WHY is the Lord sending the famine?

"Because they have not _____ to My words."

Read Leviticus 26:14-21. In verse 20 Gods tells them that their land will not yield its produce (a famine). WHY? Look at verse 14.

3. (Across) WHAT does God say? (He repeats these words throughout these verses.) "If you do not _____ Me."

Read 2 Chronicles 6:26-31. This is part of Solomon's prayer before the assembly when he finished building the temple.

4. (Down) 2 Chronicles 6:26 WHY are the heavens shut up in this verse and why is there famine in the land? "Because they have _____ against You (God)."

2 Chronicles 6:26 WHAT are the people to do?

5. (Down) _____ toward this place and

6. (Down) _____ Your name and

7. (Across) _____ from their sin.

8. (Across) 2 Chronicles 6:27 WHAT is Solomon asking God to do when He hears in heaven? _____the sin of your servants.

   2 Chronicles 6:31 WHAT are the people to do?

9. (Down) _____ You and

10. (Down) _____ in Your ways.

   Read Psalm 37:18-20.

11. (Across) WHOSE inheritance will be forever? To WHOM does God give abundance in the days of famine? The

   _____.

Our research shows us very clearly that God is the One WHO sends the famines and also tells us WHY He sends them. God allows famines because of sin and disobedience. God also provides a way for those who are blameless. Did you notice in Psalm 37 that He keeps the blameless alive? While God always judges sin, He also provides a way to preserve the righteous, and a way to bring the sinner back. If a sinner confesses his or her sin and turns back to Him, He will forgive.

Now take a look at the rebus Mr. Hetzel has been penciling for our memory verse this week. A rebus is a word puzzle that mixes pictures and words. When you combine the pictures and the letters by adding or subtracting letters, you will end up with a new word.

Solve Mr. Hetzel's creative masterpiece and write out the solution on the lines underneath the puzzle. After you have solved the rebus, don't forget to look at Genesis 45 to find the address of this verse.

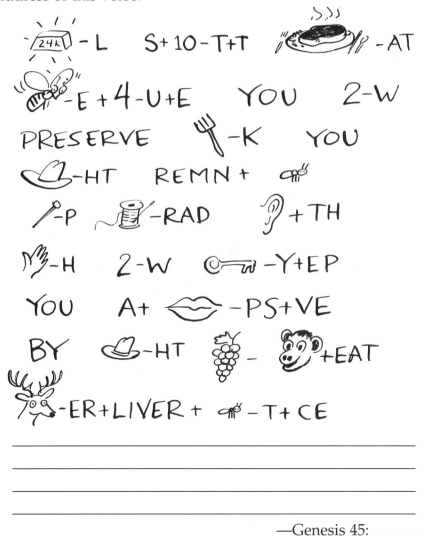

_____

_____

_____

_____

—Genesis 45: _____

BRAINSTORMING

"Hey, guys, come here quick!" Philip said as he peeked into Aunt Sherry's office. "Look at Sam."

"Oh no," Max moaned as headed toward the door. "What is he up to this time?" Max suddenly stopped as he caught a glimpse of Sam sitting in Aunt Sherry's chair with his paws on the computer keyboard and looking at her computer screen.

Molly started giggling. "Sam looks like he's writing at the computer."

"What's up, guys?" asked Aunt Sherry as she came around the corner and spotted Max, Molly, and Philip standing outside her office door looking at something. "Oh no, don't tell me. It's Sam, isn't it?"

"It sure is," Molly, replied. "Come look. Sam is the new writer for Amazing Comics."

Aunt Sherry laughed as she peeked in the doorway and caught Sam sitting in her chair and looking at the computer screen. "Come on, boy, hop down. Let's get you a nice chew stick so we can get back to work on our script." Aunt Sherry opened her bottom desk drawer and pulled out one of Sam's favorite chew sticks. Sam popped up on his hind legs, begging for his chew stick, and then he trotted over to his favorite cushion and started chewing. "Okay, guys, now that Sam is occupied we need to pull up our chairs and get out our scripts. We need to do some brainstorming. We have the setting; the famine has spread all over the face of the earth. Now grab those colored pencils. We need to find out what happens next."

Read Genesis 42 on page 133 and mark the following key words:

God (draw a purple triangle and color it yellow)

famine (box it in black and color it brown)

money (draw a green $)

die (draw a black tombstone and color it brown)

sin (color it brown)

weep (wept) (draw a blue tear)

grain (and the synonym *food*)

Also mark everything that tells you WHERE by double-underlining the WHERE in green. Mark everything that tells you WHEN with a green clock like this:

Our script is looking good. Let's make sure we have all the facts.

Genesis 42:1-5 WHAT does Jacob tell his sons to do?

_____

Genesis 42:5 WHY?

_____

Genesis 42:6 WHAT do the brothers do? (Underline this action in orange on your Observation Worksheets.)

_____

Genesis 42:7-8 Did Joseph recognize his brothers?

_____

Genesis 42:9 WHAT did Joseph remember?

_____

Did it come true?

_____

Do you see why God gave Joseph those dreams and why he told them to his brothers? Was Joseph bragging? No! Joseph was only sharing what God had shown him through his dreams. Remember, Joseph and his family did not have a Bible, so God used Joseph's dreams to show them what was going to happen.

Genesis 42:9 WHAT does Joseph accuse them of being?

_____

Genesis 42:17 WHAT did Joseph do to them?

_____

For HOW long?

_____

Genesis 42:18-20 WHAT happens in these verses?

_____

_____

_____

Genesis 42:21-24 WHAT incident do the brothers remember?

_____

Genesis 42:21 WHAT did the brothers say to one another?

"Truly we are _____ concerning our brother,

because we saw the _____ of his soul when

he_____ with us, yet we would not

_____."

Genesis 42:22 WHAT did Reuben realize?

_____

Genesis 42:24 WHAT emotion does Joseph show?

_____

Genesis 42:24 WHAT does Joseph do with Simeon?

_____

Genesis 42:25-28 WHAT does Joseph do?

_____

Genesis 42:29-34 WHAT happens in these verses?

_____

_____

Genesis 42:35-38 HOW does Jacob respond?

_____

Can you believe it? After all these years we see the brothers confessing their guilt toward Joseph. God has convicted the brothers of their sin. We also see from Reuben's response that the brothers knew God would hold them accountable for their actions. They knew that God is a holy God and that He always judges and punishes sin.

HOW about you? Have you sinned? Is God convicting you? If so, then tell God what you have done wrong. Tell Him that you are sorry and want His help not to do it again. Remember, when we confess our sin and turn away from it, Jesus will forgive us.

Joseph hears his brothers' confession and weeps. But even though the brothers have confessed their sin, Simeon is still put in jail. God always forgives us when we confess our sin, but we still have to deal with the consequences of what we did wrong. If someone cheats on a test and confesses his cheating to God, God will forgive that person for cheating, but that person will also have to deal with the consequences of cheating, like getting caught and being given a failing grade, or maybe being expelled from school. Sin still has consequences even when it is forgiven.

The brothers have returned to Canaan without Simeon, and Jacob refuses to send Benjamin back. WHAT will happen next? We'll find out as we continue to design our comic book. By the way, how is your superhero training coming along? Did you remember to practice your verse?

BREAKING DOWN THE SCRIPT

Well, guys, the comic book is really coming along. You are doing a fantastic job at developing our character by finding out what made him God's superhero. We have a lot to do today. We need to get two of our scripts broken down so Mr. Hetzel can start penciling those panels. Our deadline is getting close, and we want to make sure that this is the best comic book ever. So let's get to work. Don't forget to pray and ask God to help you as you study His Word. Then turn to page 136 and read Genesis 43 and Genesis 44. Mark the following key words for both chapters of Scripture:

God (draw a purple triangle and color it yellow)

famine (box it in black and color it brown)

money (draw a green $)

die (draw a black tombstone and color it brown)

sin (iniquity) (color it brown)

weep (wept) (draw a blue tear)

grain (and the synonym *food*)

Hebrew (draw a blue Star of David)

Also mark every time you see Joseph's brothers bowing before him (underline it in orange like you did yesterday).

Mark everything that tells you WHERE by double-underlining the WHERE in green. Mark everything that tells you WHEN with a green clock like this:

Now start breaking the script down.

Genesis 43:1-2 WHAT does Jacob ask the brothers to do?

_____

Genesis 43:8 WHO pleads with Israel (Jacob) to send Benjamin with them to Egypt?

_____

Genesis 43:9 WHAT does Judah promise his father?

_____

Now go back to Genesis 37 on page 119. Read Genesis 37:26-27.

WHOSE idea was it to sell Joseph?

_____

Isn't that incredible? Judah is the brother who wanted to sell Joseph, and now 20 years later Judah is promising his father that he will be responsible for the other favored son, Benjamin. Has Judah changed? _____ Yes _____ No

Judah has changed. Instead of trying to get rid of Jacob's other favored son, Judah is giving his oath that he will be responsible to bring Benjamin back. WHAT does this show you about God? Can God change people? Yes! Nothing is impossible with God. When we confess our sins and ask Jesus to be our Savior, God changes us.

Therefore if anyone is in Christ, he is a new creature;
the old things passed away; behold, new things have come
(2 Corinthians 5:17).

Genesis 43:11-15 WHAT did Israel tell the brothers to do?

_____

_____

Genesis 43:16 WHEN Joseph sees Benjamin, WHAT does he tell his house servant to do?

_____

Genesis 43:18 HOW did the brothers react?

_____

WHY?

_____

Genesis 43:23 WHAT did Joseph's house steward say to them?

_____

Genesis 43:26 WHAT happened when Joseph came home?

_____

Genesis 43:27 WHAT does Joseph ask them?

_____

Genesis 43:28 HOW did the brothers respond?

_____

Genesis 43:29-30 HOW did Joseph react when he saw Benjamin?

_____

Genesis 43:31-34 WHAT happens after Joseph gets control over himself?

_____

Genesis 44:1-5 WHAT does Joseph tell his house steward to do?

_____

_____

Genesis 44:6-13 WHAT happens?

_____

_____

Genesis 44:16 WHEN Joseph questions the brothers about his silver cup, WHAT is Judah's response?

"HOW can we _____ ourselves? _____

has found out the _____ of your servants."

Did Judah and the brothers take the silver cup?

_____

    Then WHY did Judah say God had found out their sin? Judah was talking about the sin they had committed against Joseph. Judah thought that God was using this situation with the silver cup to deal with their sin against Joseph.

Genesis 44:17 WHAT is Joseph's response to Judah saying they are all his slaves?

_____

_____

Joseph has told them they can all go home except Benjamin. What an opportunity! Judah could have agreed and gotten rid of Jacob's other favored son by leaving him as Joseph's slave. WHAT does Judah do?

Look at Genesis 44:18-34. WHAT is Judah doing in these verses?

_____

_____

Once again we see the change in Judah as he approaches Joseph and tells him about his father and then pleads to take Benjamin's place. Judah has come a long way from selling Joseph, participating in the lie that Joseph had been killed, and breaking his father's heart to standing up and pleading for his brother's life. Judah's plea also shows his love and concern for his father's well-being. Judah is willing to give up his life for his brother's.

Isn't that amazing? Look at what God can do when we lay aside our feelings and let Him take over. God can change the hardest heart. God can take away our anger, our bitterness, our jealousy, and our hurt. All we have to do is to turn to Him, confess our sins, and ask Him to change us.

What a superhero! Joseph has laid aside his feelings to care for his family, even though his family rejected him. Joseph chose to love and provide for them anyway.

And don't forget about Judah. He has learned to put someone else before himself. Judah was willing to sacrifice his life for his brother and father's well-being.

HOW about you?

- Will you allow God to change you? ____ Yes ____ No

- Will you be God's superhero? Will you show kindness to someone who has hurt you, instead of finding a way to get even? ____ Yes ____ No

- Are you willing to sacrifice for someone else? Share your Christmas by giving up some of your gifts and using that money to give to a needy family. Send a Christmas shoebox to Samaritan's Purse, volunteer to serve a meal in a community kitchen, or give up some of your free time to help a neighbor cut his grass. There are so many ways you can take an interest in other people and show how God has changed you.

You did it! Because of all your hard work, Mr. Hetzel can get started on those panels. This is going to be a very special comic book. Now let's head to the Bronx with Aunt Sherry, Miss Lil, Max, Molly, and Philip to see the New York Yankees play ball at Yankee Stadium. We can't wait! But before you start munching down those hot dogs, don't forget to practice saying your memory verse.

PEN, BRUSHES, AND INK

"That was an awesome ball game!" Max exclaimed.

"It sure was!" Philip agreed. "I still can't believe that you actually caught a ball in Yankee Stadium. What a souvenir!"

"That was pretty amazing," replied Aunt Sherry. "For a minute I thought we were going to be trampled by all the fans, and then I looked down and there it was—the ball was right in your hands. It was quite a thrill!"

"And the best part," Molly joined in, "was when we got to meet the players after the game and they autographed your ball."

"I know," replied Max. "I can't wait to get home and show everybody. No one is going to believe this! Good thing you had your camera, Aunt Sherry. I love New York City!"

Everybody started laughing and Aunt Sherry said, "Well, I know this won't be quite as exciting as Max's big catch, but are you guys ready to learn a new job for the comic book? The inker is ready to get started inking the panels that Mr. Hetzel has finished. Zach is going to teach you how to ink and let you practice on some of the photocopies of the sketches so you can see for yourself what it would be like to be an inker. Doesn't that sound like fun?"

"It sure does," answered Max, Molly, and Philip.

"I thought you would be excited," replied Aunt Sherry. "The first thing we need to do is to study our script to make sure Mr. Hetzel's drawings are just the way we want them before Zach starts inking."

So let's get started. Read Genesis 45 and mark the following key words:

God (draw a purple triangle and color it yellow)

famine (box it in black and color it brown)

die (draw a black tombstone and color it brown)

weep (wept) (draw a blue tear)

Mark everything that tells you WHERE by double-underlining the <u>WHERE</u> in green. Mark everything that tells you WHEN with a green clock like this:

Are you ready to meet Mr. Zach? Let's head to his office and learn how to ink the panels.

"Knock, knock," Aunt Sherry said as she tapped on Zach's office door. "I have some very excited inkers-in-training for you to meet."

"Great. Come on in, kids. Let's see, I know this is Molly, and this has to be the famous bagel-snatcher Sam, and since Philip has been here before, you must be Max." The kids laughed as Zach made the introductions. "Why don't you guys just call me Mr. Zach? Let's go over here to the drawing board. I have a place for each one of you to work—that is, except for you, Sam. You'll just have to watch today.

"Now a lot of people think that inking is such an easy job. I mean, all you have to do is trace over the penciller's lines, right? But inking a comic book is a lot more than just taking a pen or a brush and tracing over the penciller's lines. An inker needs to be an artist just like a penciller does. He or she has to know all about drawing and how to shade in areas to create different moods and contrasts.

"Inkers use different tools to ink with. They use brushes, which are the hardest tool to use, and they use dip pens with different size pen nibs so they can create different effects. Sometimes they use markers, but most inkers prefer pens and brushes with black India ink. Inkers also use different patterns such as swirls, blots, cross-hatching, broken hatching, and curlicues to give depth, add shadows, and bring the drawings to life. Take a look at this sample I did for you."

swirls   blots   cross hatching   broken hatching

curlicues   lines   stipple

So let's learn to ink. Answer the 5W's and an H below to double-check Mr. Hetzel's panels.

Genesis 45:1-2 WHAT is Joseph doing?

_____

Genesis 45:3-4 WHAT happens in these verses?

_____

Genesis 45:6 HOW long has the famine been in the land?

_____

So if Joseph was 37 years old at the beginning of the famine, HOW old would he be now?

_____

Genesis 45:5-8 WHAT does Joseph tell his brothers? WHY did God allow Joseph to be sent to Egypt?

_____

Genesis 45:8 WHO was in control of Joseph's life? WHO sent Joseph to Egypt?

_____

Genesis 45:9-13 WHAT does Joseph tell his brothers to do?

_____

Genesis 45:13-15 HOW does Joseph treat his brothers?

_____

Now look at the first panel that Mr. Hetzel has penciled, labeled Genesis 45:1-15. Tell what the main event is from these verses and write it on the lines underneath the panel. Then try your hand at being an inker. Help Mr. Zach by using a black ink pen or a marker and going over the lines in Mr. Hetzel's drawings to ink the first panel. Be creative and add some of Mr. Zach's special touches.

Now, after you have finished writing the main thing and inking the first panel, look at the next panel, labeled Genesis 45:16-20. Write the main thing that is happening in these verses and ink the second panel. Then do the same thing for the other two panels, #3 and #4.

Genesis 45:1-15

Genesis 45:16-20

Genesis 45:17-24

Genesis 45:25-28

Incredible! Look at God's superhero. After all these years, the moment of truth arrives. WHAT does Joseph do once he is reunited with his brothers? He weeps. He cries so loudly that everyone hears him. Then he looks at his brothers. Oh boy, here it comes—payback time. Does Joseph say, "Guess what, guys? It's your brother Joseph. You know—the one you wanted to kill, the one you threw into a pit and sold as a slave. Well, I'm not a slave anymore. I'm second in command, and it is time for you to pay for all the pain and suffering you caused me."

No way! Instead, Joseph says, "Do not be grieved or angry with yourselves." Can you believe it? After the way they mistreated him, he is concerned about how they are feeling! HOW can he do that? HOW can Joseph show such love and compassion? Another character trait is revealed:

CHARACTER TRAIT #8: FORGIVENESS

Forgiveness means "to send away." It is not holding a grudge against the person who committed a wrongdoing. It is to set the person free without any resentment. It is to excuse the offender. Forgiveness is not getting even. Joseph is a man of forgiveness. He does not take revenge on his brothers for their wrongdoing. He is full of love and compassion instead of bitterness and resentment.

> WHAT would you have done if you were Joseph? Would you want revenge? Would you be angry and bitter? Or would you forgive? Write out what you would do if you were treated like Joseph.

_____

_____

> WHOM did Joseph recognize as being in control of his circumstances?

_____

Isn't our superhero amazing? Joseph knew that God was in control of his circumstances. He even told his brothers WHY God allowed him to be sold to Egypt. He was sent to Egypt to keep them alive during the famine. God was looking ahead, planning for their welfare. God took the bad, the ugly, and the hurtful in Joseph's life and used it for good. Now go back to page 12 and write out WHY God allowed this to happen to Joseph on his character profile. WHAT was Joseph's mission?

Joseph saw God at work. He had a superhero's faith. He chose to trust God rather than his circumstances. HOW about you? Do you trust God completely, no matter what happens? Do you have a superhero's faith?

EXAMINE THE ART

"You did an awesome job inking those sketches!" Aunt Sherry said as we munched on bagels and cream cheese in her office. "Yesterday Jacob found out that Joseph is alive. Can you imagine what it will be like for this father to finally see his loved and favorite son after thinking he was dead all these years?" HOW do you think our superhero will react when he finally sees his father? WHAT did Joseph do when he was reunited with his brothers? Will he weep when he sees Jacob? Let's find out as we compare our script to Mr. Hetzel's art to make sure his drawings have captured the mood of this emotional scene.

Let's read Genesis 46 and Genesis 47 and mark the following key words:

God (draw a purple triangle and color it yellow)

famine (box it in black and color it brown)

die (draw a black tombstone and color it brown)

grain (and the synonym *food*)

blessed (blessing) (draw a blue cloud around it and color it pink)

money (draw a green $)

Mark everything that tells you WHERE by double-underlining the <u>WHERE</u> in green. Mark everything that tells you WHEN with a green clock like this: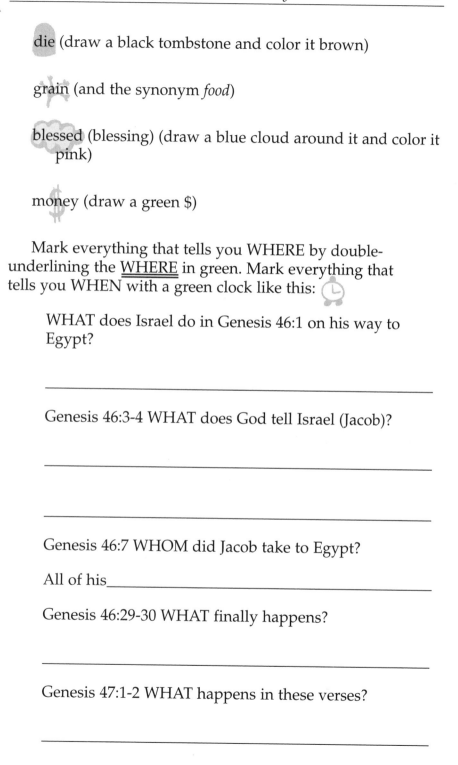

WHAT does Israel do in Genesis 46:1 on his way to Egypt?

_____

Genesis 46:3-4 WHAT does God tell Israel (Jacob)?

_____

_____

Genesis 46:7 WHOM did Jacob take to Egypt?

All of his_____

Genesis 46:29-30 WHAT finally happens?

_____

Genesis 47:1-2 WHAT happens in these verses?

_____

Genesis 47:6 WHAT does Pharaoh tell Joseph?

_____

Genesis 47:7 WHAT does Jacob do?

_____

Genesis 47:11 WHAT does Joseph do?

_____

Genesis 47:14 WHAT did Joseph do with the money?

_____

Genesis 47:16-17 WHAT did the Egyptians exchange for food when their money was gone?

_____

_____

Genesis 47:18-23 HOW did the Egyptians pay Joseph the next year?

_____

_____

Genesis 47:24 WHAT were they to give Pharaoh at the harvest?

_____

Genesis 47:25 HOW did the Egyptians respond?

_____

Genesis 47:27 WHAT happened to Joseph's family in Egypt?

_____

Genesis 47:29-31 WHAT does Israel ask Joseph to do?

_____

Wow—what a caravan! God moves Jacob's entire family to Egypt. WHAT if God wanted your family to move? Would you be willing to go? Would you be afraid? Would it be hard to leave your friends behind?

Just remember: Sometimes God changes our lives. He changes our school, or our neighborhood, and maybe even our city or state. We need to trust that God knows what is best for us. We need to remember that God moved Joseph in order to save a nation. Did you notice how the people responded to Joseph? They told him, "You have saved our lives." Are you willing for God to put you wherever He thinks is best so that He can use you?

4
A SUPERHERO FORGIVES

GENESIS 48–50

"Now this is a park!" Molly exclaimed as she, Max, Sam, and Philip headed into Central Park with Aunt Sherry and Miss Lil.

Aunt Sherry smiled and asked, "What do you want to do first: rent bicycles, check out the carousel, watch the boats, or have our picnic?"

"How about going to Conservatory Water to the model boat pond?" asked Philip. He looked at Molly and Max to explain, "That's the pond that has all the remote-controlled mini yachts."

"Yeah, that sounds like fun. Let's do that," replied Max.

"Okay," Aunt Sherry said. "And after we watch the boats, we can throw Frisbees, eat our picnic lunch, and get some ice cream for dessert. Let's go play in the park!"

pLaciNG OUR paNELS

"Aunt Sherry, don't you think you can talk Dad into moving us to New York City? After all, you are his baby sister," Max said as he plopped down on the blanket next to Aunt Sherry.

Aunt Sherry laughed. "It would be great having you live here, Max, but I don't think your dad will go for that. You can come back to visit anytime you want to. And since this is your last week here, Lil and I have decided instead of rushing back to the office, we can work on the comic book out here."

"That's a great idea," Max, Philip, and Molly replied.

"Let's grab some ice cream at the Ice Cream Cafe, and then we can sit on our blanket and get to work."

As we get started on our comic book, let's do a quick review to put ourselves back in context. Look up and read Acts 7:8-16. Now look at our comic book panels on the next page. Each panel is a scene from Joseph's life, but they are all mixed up. You need to look at the comic book panels drawn on the left side and match them to the description on the right. Then number each panel from 1 to 6 to put each event in the correct order that it happened.

Panel #
____   Pharaoh sets Joseph over Egypt/gives ring, necklace, and chariot

Panel #
____   Jacob and Joseph reunited

Panel #
____   Joseph thrown into the pit

Panel #
____   Joseph as Potiphar's slave fleeing temptation

Panel #
____   Joseph's brothers bow before him

Panel #
____   Joseph in jail with cupbearer and chief baker

Great work! Now head back to our script on page 149 and read Genesis 48. Mark the following key words:

God (draw a purple triangle and color it yellow)

blessed (blessing) (draw a blue cloud around it and color it pink)

Manasseh (color it orange)

Ephraim (color it blue)

Mark everything that tells you WHERE by double-underlining the <u>WHERE</u> in green. Mark everything that tells you WHEN with a green clock like this:

Genesis 48:1 WHY does Joseph go to Jacob?

_____

Genesis 48:3 WHAT does Jacob tell Joseph about God?

_____

Genesis 48:4 WHAT was the blessing?

_____

_____

Genesis 48:5-6 WHAT does Jacob tell Joseph about Ephraim and Manasseh?

_____

Genesis 48:8-14 WHAT does Israel do?

_____

Genesis 48:15 WHAT does Israel say about Abraham and Isaac?

They _____ before God.

WHAT does Israel say about God?

_____

Genesis 48:17-18 WHY is Joseph displeased?

_____

Genesis 48:19 WHAT did Israel say about the boys? WHO will be greater—the younger or the older?

_____

Genesis 48:21-22 WHAT does Israel tell Joseph?

_____

_____

Now let's go rent some bikes for a ride through the park.

PULLING IT TOGETHER—MORE RESEARCH

We had a great time in Central Park. There is so much to see and do. But today we need to head back to Amazing Comics and pull our story together by doing a little more research. Yesterday we saw that when Israel blessed Joseph, he talked about God "as the God before whom my fathers Abraham and Isaac walked." Isn't that wonderful to see what a rich heritage Joseph had? His family walked with God. Today let's do some cross-references to see what we can find out about walking with God. Talk with your Master Editor, and then look up and read the following verses to solve the crossword puzzle below.

1. (Down) Genesis 6:9 Noah walked with God. HOW was Noah described? Noah was a _____ man,

2. (Across) _____ in his time.

3. (Down) Deuteronomy 30:15-16 HOW did Moses command the children of Israel to walk? Walk in His _____.

4. (Down) To keep His _____ and His statutes and His judgments.

5. (Down) Deuteronomy 30:16 WHAT was the result from walking with God? "The Lord your God may _____ you in the land where you are entering to possess it."

6. (Down) Micah 6:8 HOW did Micah tell Israel to walk? Walk _____ with your God.

7. (Across) 1 John 1:5-7 HOW do we walk if we have fellowship with one another and the blood of Jesus cleanses us from all sin?
"We walk in the _____."

8. (Down) 1 John 2:4-6 HOW are we to walk if we abide in Him (Jesus)?
We are to walk in the same _____ as He walked.

9. (Across) WHO is this He? WHOM are we to abide in? WHO died for our sins (1 John 2:1-2)? _____
Ephesians 4:1-3 HOW are you to walk?

10. (Across) In a manner _____ of the calling with which you have been called, with all

11. (Across) _____, and

12. (Across) _____, with

13. (Down)_____, showing

14. (Across) _____ for one another in love, being diligent to preserve the

15. (Across) _____ of the Spirit in the bond of peace.

16. (Across) Ephesians 5:1-2 Walk in _____.

Ephesians 5:15-17

17. (Down) Be _____ how you walk.

18. (Across) Walk as _____ men.

Now that we have done our research and have seen what it means to walk with God, did Joseph walk with God? ____ Yes ____ No

HOW about you? WHAT is your walk like?

- Do you walk in God's ways? Do you keep His commandments? Do you obey God? ____ Yes ____ No

- Do you walk humbly? Have you bowed the knee and surrendered yourself to God? Or have you put yourself in God's place?

  _____

- Do you walk in the light?
  Do you tell the truth? ____ Yes ____ No
  Do you love other people? ____ Yes ____ No

- Do you walk like Jesus? Jesus sacrificed His life for others. He did God's will, not His. He chose to put other people before Himself. Name a way that you walk like Jesus:

  _____

- Do you walk in a manner worthy of your calling? Do people see patience, gentleness, and humility in you? ____ Yes ____ No

- Are you careful how you walk? Are you wise? Do you know God's Word? ____ Yes ____ No

Be like Joseph—become God's superhero by walking with Him!

Now take a look at the maze of word balloons that Marie has created below. There is only one way to connect each word balloon from start to finish. Find your way through the maze by coloring each word balloon that is connected to another word balloon in order to find the correct path and uncover your memory verse.

Start

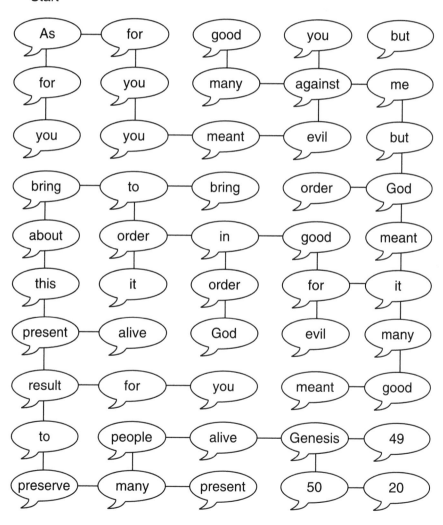

Finish

Now practice your lettering. Write this verse on an index card and say it aloud three times in a row, three times today!

BE THE COLORIST

"Can you believe it? We are in the final stages of designing our comic book," Aunt Sherry announced to Max, Molly, and Philip as they headed down the hallway with Sam. "The next stage is to add the color to the inked pages. Today our colorist, Allyce, is going to show you how to color our work of art."

"Hi, Allyce. This is Max and Molly, and I believe you already know Lil's son, Philip."

"Hi, guys. Are you ready to learn how to be a colorist for a comic book? Come over here and take a look. The first thing a colorist does is to take photocopies of the original artwork and pick out the colors that will be used in the comic book by using a computer color separator. The color separator gives us a color guide that has all the possible hues of color.

"Then the colorist will paint the photocopy using different kinds of dyes, watercolors, acrylic paints, colored pencils, or oils to the get the effect he wants. Once it's finished, the colorist will take an ink pen and put a dot in the center of each colored area and draw a line to the outside margin, writing the color code for that color.

"The computer separator will scan in reduced black-and-white images from the original artwork, so the computer technician will be able to put the color in the right place by looking at what color goes with each dot. Once the technician is finished, a color key will be printed for the editor and the colorist to look over to check for any mistakes. After that, a press test is done, and if the press test is given the okay, the comic book will be sent to the printer."

"Wow, that is so awesome," Max said. "I can't wait! Let's get to work!"

So are you ready to be the colorist? Let's get started by reading Genesis 49 on page 151, and marking the following key words:

God (draw a purple triangle and color it yellow)

Every reference to the sons of Israel:
  Reuben, Simeon, Levi, Judah, Zebulun, Issachar, Dan, Gad, Asher, Naphtali, Joseph, and Benjamin (color each one blue)

Blessed (blessing) (put a blue cloud around it and color it pink)

Mark everything that tells you WHERE by double-underlining the WHERE in green. Mark everything that tells you WHEN with a green clock like this:

Genesis 49:1-2 WHAT is happening? WHAT is Jacob doing?

_____

Genesis 49:3-28 WHICH two sons receive the longest blessing?

_____

Usually the firstborn son received the birthright. WHO was Jacob's firstborn? If you don't remember look back on page 16.

_____

Look up and read 1 Chronicles 5:1-2. WHOM was Israel's birthright given to?

_____

Even though Reuben was the firstborn son, God didn't give him the birthright because of his sin.

Genesis 49:22-26 WHAT do we learn about Joseph? HOW is he described? Joseph is a _____ bough by a spring.

WHAT happened when he was attacked?
His bow _____ _____.

Genesis 49:26 WHAT do you see about Joseph and his brothers?
Joseph was d __ __ __ __ __ __ __ __ __ __ __ __ among his brothers.

That's what superheroes are—they are distinguished, they are known for excellence in their conduct and character. We never see Joseph disobeying God.

WHAT do we see about God in these same verses?

_____

_____

Genesis 49:8-12 WHAT do we learn about Judah?

His brothers shall _____ him.

His hand will be on the _____ of

his_____.

His father's sons shall _____ _____

to him.

He is a _____ whelp.

The _____ shall not depart from him. He is

the ruler until _____ comes.

The word *Shiloh* is a form of the Hebrew expression which means "one to whom it belongs." So we see that the scepter, the rulership, will belong to Judah until the one to whom it (the rulership) belongs comes. WHO do you think this one is? _____

Look up and read Isaiah 9:6-7. WHO is this child that Isaiah is prophesying will have the government rest on His shoulders?

_____

Look up and read Matthew 1:1-6. WHOSE genealogy is this?

_____

WHAT tribe of Israel will Jesus come from?

_____

WHAT other king do you see listed in this genealogy?
King D ___ ___ ___ ___

Look up and read Matthew 2:5-6.
WHAT will come out of the land of Judah?

_____

Look up and read Revelation 19:15-16.
WHAT do we learn about Jesus when He comes again to rule the earth? WHAT comes out of His mouth?

_____

WHAT will He do with it?

_____

HOW will He rule?

_____

WHAT name is written on His robe?

_____

Isn't this exciting? One day Jesus will come again, and when He does, every knee will bow and every tongue will declare that He is the Lord. Have you bowed the knee? Is Jesus Christ the Lord of your life? Have you turned over the rulership to Him?

How awesome to see Jacob as he gathers his sons together and tells them what will happen to them in the days to come. Did you notice that he gave each son a blessing that was appropriate to him? We saw that Reuben did not receive the firstborn's inheritance because of his sin. Judah received the blessing of leadership, and Jesus the Messiah (the Christ) would come through the tribe of Judah. Joseph's blessing was one of fruitfulness and being distinguished among his brothers.

Look at Genesis 49:33. As Jacob finishes blessing his sons, WHAT happens?

_____

Now become the colorist. Color these two panels from Genesis 49:

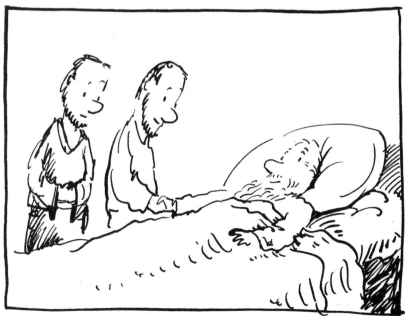

You are becoming quite an artist!

PENCiLiNG, iNKiNG, AND COLORiNG

"Hey, guys, how did you like working with Allyce?" Aunt Sherry asked.

"It was great! I never really knew how much work it takes to put out a comic book," Molly answered.

"It's quite a process," Aunt Sherry responded, "but as you can see, it's a lot of fun. Today we are going to work on the last chapter of Genesis. Our superhero's story is coming to an end, but it's only the beginning of the history of Israel. Seventy people have left their promised land in Canaan to live in the land of Egypt. WHAT happens after Jacob dies? Let's pull out our scripts and work on the ending for our comic book."

Read Genesis 50 on page 155 and mark the following key words:

God (draw a purple triangle and color it yellow)

Joseph's brothers bowing before him (underline in orange)

die (draw a black tombstone and color it brown)

weep (wept) (draw a blue tear)

transgression (color it brown)

forgive (circle it in red)

afraid (draw blue squiggles above and below the word)

bury (draw a brown shovel)

Mark everything that tells you <u>WHERE</u> by double-underlining the WHERE in green. Mark everything that tells you WHEN with a green clock like this:

Genesis 50:1-3 WHAT happens in these verses?

_____

_____

Genesis 50:4-6 WHAT does Joseph do after the days of mourning are past?

_____

Genesis 50:7-10 WHO went with Joseph to bury his father?

_____

_____

Genesis 50:10 WHERE does Joseph observe seven days of mourning?

_____

Genesis 50:13 WHERE did Jacob's sons carry him?

_____

Genesis 50:13 WHERE is Jacob buried?

_____

Now become the penciller, inker, and colorist. Draw Joseph and company carrying Jacob to the cave in the box below. Ink it in and color it with your colored pencils.

Genesis 50:14 WHAT did Joseph do after he buried Jacob?

_____

What a masterpiece! Tomorrow we will finish our comic book as we find out what happens after Joseph returns to Egypt.

THE FINISHING TOUCHES

"Surprise!" yelled the staff at Amazing Comics as Max, Molly, Sam, and Philip walked inside the conference room to meet with Aunt Sherry. Sam went haywire barking as the kids stood still with shocked looks on their faces.

"Come on, Sam, calm down. It's just us," Aunt Sherry laughed as she tried to calm a very excited Sam.

Max was the first to ask, "What's going on?"

Miss Lil walked up to the kids and explained. "Since this is your last day at Amazing Comics, we wanted to have a going-away party just for you. You have worked so hard and learned so much. We are so proud of you! We even have some art supplies for you to take home so you can make your own comic book."

"Oh, wow, this is so cool! Thanks," replied Max, Molly, and Philip.

"Okay, let's eat," Aunt Sherry called out. "We still have a deadline. We need to put those final touches on the comic book."

Grab those scripts. Joseph has buried Jacob and returned to Egypt along with his brothers and the rest of those who went with him. Turn to pages 155-157 and read Genesis 50:15-26.

Genesis 50:15 WHAT is Joseph's brothers' concern after their father dies?

_____

Genesis 50:16 WHAT do they do?

_____

Genesis 50:17 WHAT do they ask Joseph to do?

_____

HOW does Joseph respond?

_____

Genesis 50:18 WHAT do the brothers do?

_____

Genesis 50:19-20 WHAT does Joseph say?

_____

WHO is in control?

_____

WHY did God allow it to happen?

_____

Genesis 50:21 WHAT does Joseph do?

_____

Now be the penciller and the colorist. Draw and color this panel on Genesis 50:15-21 on page 108.

Isn't that amazing? Our superhero not only forgives his brothers, but he comforts them, speaks kindly to them, and provides for their children. HOW is Joseph able to forgive the brothers who hurt and rejected him? Joseph knew God. He recognized that even though his brothers wanted to hurt him, he was in God's hands. God had allowed his brothers to sell him to Egypt so that He could save a nation. Joseph had a superhero's trust in an almighty God. The reason we never see Joseph angry or bitter is because he forgave the wrongs that were done to him. That's what makes him a superhero. Joseph is like Jesus—he forgave, just like Jesus did.

Let's look at some cross-references to see what God's Word has to say about forgiveness.

Look up and read Colossians 2:13-14. WHAT did Jesus do when we were dead in our transgressions?

He made us _____ together with Him.

He has _____ us all our transgressions.

He _____ out the certificate of _____.

Ephesians 4:32 HOW are we to treat one another?

_____

_____

WHY?

_____

Colossians 3:12-13 HOW are those who are chosen of God to behave?

_____

_____

_____

Matthew 6:9-15 WHAT happens if we forgive others for their transgressions?

_____

WHAT happens if we don't forgive?

_____

Matthew 18:21-22 HOW many times should we forgive?

_____

Do you see how important forgiveness is? God's Word shows us very clearly that we are to forgive because Jesus has forgiven us. It doesn't mean that you will be able to forget what happened, and it doesn't mean that the person who wronged you won't be punished. It means that you are handing what they did to you over to God, and that you will let God be their judge. You will not hold their offense against them; you will let it go; you will set them free.

If there is someone you need to forgive, such as a group of kids who have left you out or someone who has made fun of you, then write that person's name out below and tell what he or she did to you.

I need to forgive _____

because _____

_____

Now go to God and tell Him whom you need to forgive and why. Tell Him that you can't do it, but you know He can do it through you. Turn your hurt and anger over to Him. Remember: God is in control, and He is using this for your good, just like He did for Joseph. Trust God and lean on His promises in Romans 8:28:

> _And we know that God causes all things to work together for good to those who love God, to those who are called according to His purpose._

Did you notice that God didn't say that all things are good, but that He causes all things to work for good?

Be like Joseph. Put on an attitude of forgiveness, and allow God's superpower to work in you!

Now let's put the finishing touches on our comic book.

Genesis 50:24 WHAT does Joseph tell his brothers?

_____

_____

Genesis 50:25 WHEN they left Egypt, WHAT were they to take with them?

_____

Genesis 50:26 HOW old was Joseph when he died?

_____

Look up and read Genesis 15:13-16.

Genesis 15:13 WHAT did God tell Abraham about his descendants?

Your descendants will be _____ in a land that is not theirs.

WHERE are the children of Israel at the end of Genesis 50? Are they in the promised land (Canaan)?

_____

Genesis 15:13 WHAT will happen to them in Egypt?

_____

HOW long?

_____

Genesis 15:14 WHAT will God do?

_____

WHAT will happen after God judges the nation?

_____

As we look at the passages in Genesis 15, we see that God told Abraham what would happen. His descendants, the children of Israel, would be strangers in a land that wasn't theirs (Egypt), and they would be enslaved and oppressed for 400 years, but God would bring them back to their promised land. As Joseph dies, he comforts his brothers and reminds them of what God told Abraham would happen to them and of God's promise to bring them out of Egypt and back to the promised land.

Now be the inker and the colorist for the last time. Draw this panel of Joseph's death in Genesis 50:26 below.

Genesis 50:15-21	Genesis 50:26

Awesome artwork! You have just finished the comic book! Now grab your family or friends to play a drawing game on the life of our superhero. You will need some small slips of paper, two pencils, plain white paper to draw on, and a bowl.

Write down different scenes from our comic book on the small slips of paper. We have listed some ideas for you below. After you have written down your ideas, fold the pieces of paper up and put them in the bowl. Divide your family or friends into two teams. Choose someone from the first team to pick one of the slips from the bowl.

This person will have one minute to draw whatever is written on the paper for his teammates. While he is drawing, have his teammates call out what they think he is drawing while the other team times them. If they guess the right answer before their minute is up, they get 100 points for their team. If they haven't guessed it and time is up, the other team gets to make one guess. If the guess is correct, they get the 100 points.

Then it's the second team's turn to choose a slip out of the bowl to draw. Go back and forth between both teams until you run out of pieces of paper, and whoever has the most points wins!

DRAWING IDEAS

Jacob giving Joseph his varicolored tunic

Joseph's dreams

Joseph being thrown into the pit

Joseph sold as a slave

Joseph's brothers showing Jacob his bloodstained tunic

Joseph fleeing Potipher's wife and leaving his garment behind

Joseph thrown in jail

The cupbearer's dream

The chief baker's dream

Pharaoh's birthday feast with the cupbearer putting the cup in Pharaoh's hand

Death of chief baker

Pharaoh's first dream

Pharaoh's second dream

Joseph set over Egypt and given a ring, garments, gold necklace, and chariot

Joseph gathering the grain and storing it

Famine in the land

Joseph's brothers bowing before him

Joseph puts his brothers in jail

Joseph weeping

Joseph's house steward searching the brothers' bags and finding the silver cup

Joseph reveals himself to his brothers

Joseph and Jacob reunited

Jacob's blessing

Jacob dies and is carried to Canaan

Joseph's death—he is placed in a coffin in Egypt

HEROES ANYONE?

You did it! We can't wait to see the very first copy of our comic book. It is going to be one action-packed adventure! But more importantly, every kid will discover what made Joseph God's superhero. Joseph didn't have superpowers or might; it was all about God, WHO was ruling his life.

WHO rules your life? Have you given your life to Jesus Christ? Have you asked God to forgive your sins? Are you ready to follow Him?

Your hard work really paid off! Look at all you have discovered about Joseph's character that made him God's superhero. He was a man of integrity and faith. Joseph was hurt, rejected by his family, and put in jail for 13 years for something he didn't do. But he never complained, he never said it wasn't fair. Instead, he showed love and compassion, he humbled himself, he endured, and he forgave. Joseph allowed God to mold him into His superhero so that he could be used to save a nation.

Not only did we get to see our superhero in action, but we also saw the character of God. God is omnipresent; He is always there. God never left Joseph. Even in the hard and difficult times, He extended His kindness to him. God was in control. He is sovereign. He kept Joseph's brothers from killing him, He gave the dreams and the interpretations, He took Joseph from a prison to a palace, He sent the famine, and He saved a nation. God is all-powerful, He is faithful, He is gracious and merciful, and God forgives.

We also saw our superhero leave his brothers with a promise of hope as he dies. God has given us a promise, too. WHO is coming one day very soon? We need to be ready. We need to be like Joseph. We need to be God's superhero. Do you have what it takes? Yes, if you have put your faith in Jesus. All it takes are faith, obedience, and perseverance (not giving up).

Are you allowing God to work in you? Are you going to keep studying God's Word? We are so proud of you for doing these Bible studies. You are on your way to being a superhero of the faith!

Don't forget to fill out the card in the back of the book. We want to send you a special certificate for helping us search out truth and discover what made Joseph God's superhero.

Now let's go grab some hero sandwiches for our last picnic in Central Park. And don't forget to keep your eyes on Sam. You know how he loves to eat. We hate to say good-bye to New York City; we have had so much fun! See you for another adventure in God's Word real soon!

Molly, Max, and

(Sam)

P.S. Now that you have helped create our comic book, maybe you would like to make a comic book of your very own.

JUST FOR FUN: CREATE YOUR OWN COMIC BOOK

You will need:

art paper (twice the size of a comic-book page)
markers, colored pencils, or watercolors
pencils and pens
glue
staples
masking tape

To create your comic book, you need to sit down and think of some ideas that you would like your comic book to be about. You might want to make your comic book about a time when you acted like a superhero. Write out your story and think of ways to show your story in pictures. Then get your swipes, your pictures, magazines, and books to help you know how to draw some of the things you are writing about. There are also some great books at the library that will show how to draw comic books. Once you are ready, start sketching each panel for your book.

The reason we suggest that you use art paper that is twice the size of a comic-book page is so you will be able to draw two pages on one side of the sheet and then fold it in half to get two pages of your comic book.

Also take two pages of your artwork and glue the two blank sides together so that you can show your artwork on both sides of the paper. Once your sketches are complete, be the inker and the colorist. Use watercolors, colored pencils, or markers to create your masterpiece, but be careful! Don't smear your artwork. And don't forget to create a front cover for your book.

Once your pages are glued together, put them in order, fold them, and use a stapler to staple the pages on the left side. You will probably need to use three or four staples. Then cut a piece of masking tape lengthwise so it will cover your staples and be the binding for your book. Have fun! You have just created your very own comic book!

LET'S BEGIN

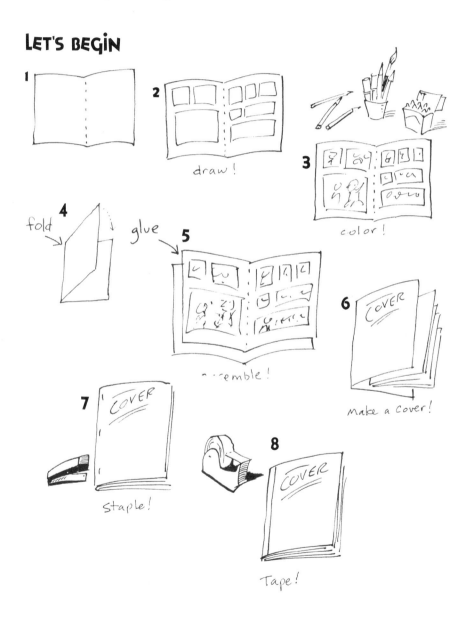

PUZZLE ANSWERS

Page 13

Now Israel <u>loved</u> Joseph <u>more</u> than all his <u>sons</u>, because he was the son of his old age; and he made him a <u>varicolored</u> <u>tunic</u>. His <u>brothers</u> saw that their <u>father</u> loved him more than all his brothers; and so they <u>hated</u> him and could not <u>speak</u> to him on friendly terms.

—Genesis 37:3-4

Page 32

But the
Lord was with
Joseph and extended
kindness to him,
and gave him favor
in the sight of
the chief jailer.
Genesis 39:21

Page 50

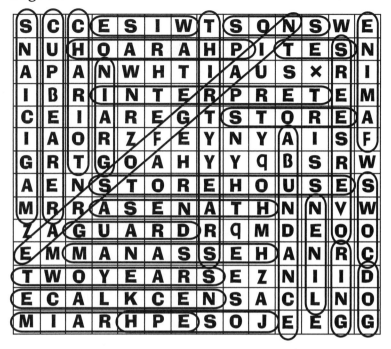

Page 62

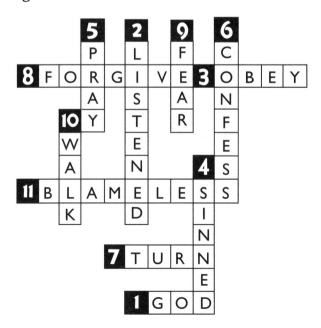

Page 63

God sent me before you to preserve for you a remnant in the earth, and to keep you alive by a great deliverance.

—Genesis 45:7

Page 87

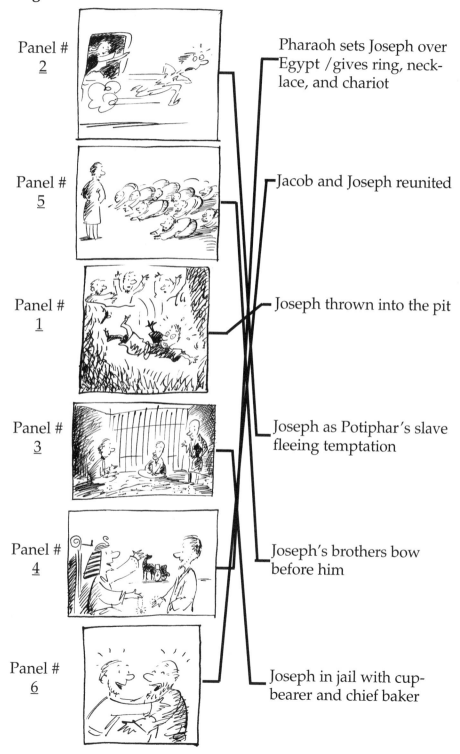

Panel #
<u>2</u>

Panel #
<u>5</u>

Panel #
<u>1</u>

Panel #
<u>3</u>

Panel #
<u>4</u>

Panel #
<u>6</u>

Pharaoh sets Joseph over Egypt /gives ring, necklace, and chariot

Jacob and Joseph reunited

Joseph thrown into the pit

Joseph as Potiphar's slave fleeing temptation

Joseph's brothers bow before him

Joseph in jail with cup-bearer and chief baker

Page 90

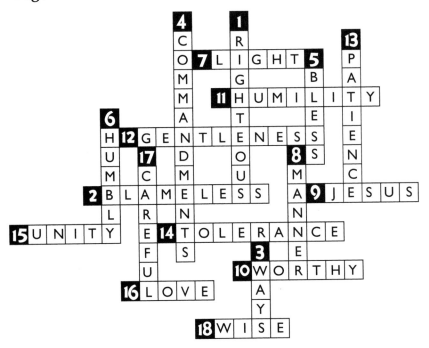

Page 93

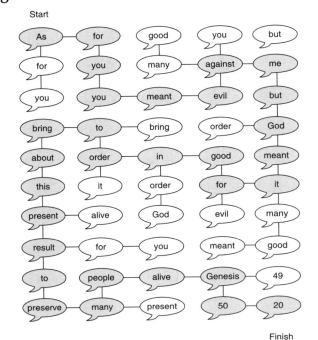

OBSERVATION WORKSHEETS
GENESIS 37-50

Chapter 37

1   Now Jacob lived in the land where his father had sojourned, in the land of Canaan.

2   These are the records of the generations of Jacob.

Joseph, when seventeen years of age, was pasturing the flock with his brothers while he was still a youth, along with the sons of Bilhah and the sons of Zilpah, his father's wives. And Joseph brought back a bad report about them to their father.

3   Now Israel loved Joseph more than all his sons, because he was the son of his old age; and he made him a varicolored tunic.

4   His brothers saw that their father loved him more than all his brothers; and so they hated him and could not speak to him on friendly terms.

5   Then Joseph had a dream, and when he told it to his brothers, they hated him even more.

6   He said to them, "Please listen to this dream which I have had;

7   for behold, we were binding sheaves in the field, and lo, my sheaf rose up and also stood erect; and behold, your sheaves gathered around and bowed down to my sheaf."

8   Then his brothers said to him, "Are you actually going to reign over us? Or are you really going to rule over us?" So they hated him even more for his dreams and for his words.

9   Now he had still another dream, and related it to his brothers, and said, "Lo, I have had still another dream; and behold, the sun and the moon and eleven stars were bowing down to me."

10   He related it to his father and to his brothers; and his father rebuked him and said to him, "What is this dream that you have had? Shall I and

your mother and your brothers actually come to bow ourselves down before you to the ground?"

11   His brothers were jealous of him, but his father kept the saying in mind.

12   Then his brothers went to pasture their father's flock in Shechem.

13   Israel said to Joseph, "Are not your brothers pasturing the flock in Shechem? Come, and I will send you to them." And he said to him, "I will go."

14   Then he said to him, "Go now and see about the welfare of your brothers and the welfare of the flock, and bring word back to me." So he sent him from the valley of Hebron, and he came to Shechem.

15   A man found him, and behold, he was wandering in the field; and the man asked him, "What are you looking for?"

16   He said, "I am looking for my brothers; please tell me where they are pasturing the flock."

17   Then the man said, "They have moved from here; for I heard them say, 'Let us go to Dothan.'" So Joseph went after his brothers and found them at Dothan.

18   When they saw him from a distance and before he came close to them, they plotted against him to put him to death.

19   They said to one another, "Here comes this dreamer!

20   Now then, come and let us kill him and throw him into one of the pits; and we will say, 'A wild beast devoured him.' Then let us see what will become of his dreams!"

21   But Reuben heard this and rescued him out of their hands and said, "Let us not take his life."

22   Reuben further said to them, "Shed no blood. Throw him into this pit that is in the wilderness, but do not lay hands on him"—that he might rescue him out of their hands, to restore him to his father.

23   So it came about, when Joseph reached his brothers, that they stripped Joseph of his tunic, the varicolored tunic that was on him;

24   and they took him and threw him into the pit. Now the pit was empty, without any water in it.

25   Then they sat down to eat a meal. And as they raised their eyes and looked, behold, a caravan of Ishmaelites was coming from Gilead, with their camels bearing aromatic gum and balm and myrrh, on their way to bring them down to Egypt.

26   Judah said to his brothers, "What profit is it for us to kill our brother and cover up his blood?

27   "Come and let us sell him to the Ishmaelites and not lay our hands on him, for he is our brother, our own flesh." And his brothers listened to him.

28   Then some Midianite traders passed by, so they pulled him up and lifted Joseph out of the pit, and sold him to the Ishmaelites for twenty shekels of silver. Thus they brought Joseph into Egypt.

29   Now Reuben returned to the pit, and behold, Joseph was not in the pit; so he tore his garments.

30   He returned to his brothers and said, "The boy is not there; as for me, where am I to go?"

31   So they took Joseph's tunic, and slaughtered a male goat and dipped the tunic in the blood;

32   and they sent the varicolored tunic and brought it to their father and said, "We found this; please examine it to see whether it is your son's tunic or not."

33   Then he examined it and said, "It is my son's tunic. A wild beast has devoured him; Joseph has surely been torn to pieces!"

34   So Jacob tore his clothes, and put sackcloth on his loins and mourned for his son many days.

35   Then all his sons and all his daughters arose to comfort him, but he refused to be comforted. And he said, "Surely I will go down to Sheol in mourning for my son." So his father wept for him.

36 Meanwhile, the Midianites sold him in Egypt to Potiphar, Pharaoh's officer, the captain of the bodyguard.

Chapter 38

1   And it came about at that time, that Judah departed from his brothers and visited a certain Adullamite, whose name was Hirah.

2   Judah saw there a daughter of a certain Canaanite whose name was Shua; and he took her and went in to her.

3   So she conceived and bore a son and he named him Er.

4   Then she conceived again and bore a son and named him Onan.

5   She bore still another son and named him Shelah; and it was at Chezib that she bore him.

6   Now Judah took a wife for Er his firstborn, and her name was Tamar.

7   But Er, Judah's firstborn, was evil in the sight of the LORD, so the LORD took his life.

8   Then Judah said to Onan, "Go in to your brother's wife, and perform your duty as a brother-in-law to her, and raise up offspring for your brother."

9   Onan knew that the offspring would not be his; so when he went in to his brother's wife, he wasted his seed on the ground in order not to give offspring to his brother.

10   But what he did was displeasing in the sight of the LORD; so He took his life also.

11   Then Judah said to his daughter-in-law Tamar, "Remain a widow in your father's house until my son Shelah grows up"; for he thought, "I am afraid that he too may die like his brothers." So Tamar went and lived in her father's house.

12   Now after a considerable time Shua's daughter, the wife of Judah, died; and when the time of mourning was ended, Judah went up to his sheepshearers at Timnah, he and his friend Hirah the Adullamite.

13   It was told to Tamar, "Behold, your father-in-law is going up to Timnah to shear his sheep."

14   So she removed her widow's garments and covered herself with a veil, and wrapped herself, and sat in the gateway of Enaim, which is on the road to Timnah; for she saw that Shelah had grown up, and she had not been given to him as a wife.

15   When Judah saw her, he thought she was a harlot, for she had covered her face.

16   So he turned aside to her by the road, and said, "Here now, let me come in to you"; for he did not know that she was his daughter-in-law. And she said, "What will you give me, that you may come in to me?"

17   He said, therefore, "I will send you a young goat from the flock." She said, moreover, "Will you give a pledge until you send it?"

18   He said, "What pledge shall I give you?" And she said, "Your seal and your cord, and your staff that is in your hand." So he gave them to her and went in to her, and she conceived by him.

19   Then she arose and departed, and removed her veil and put on her widow's garments.

20   When Judah sent the young goat by his friend the Adullamite, to receive the pledge from the woman's hand, he did not find her.

21   He asked the men of her place, saying, "Where is the temple prostitute who was by the road at Enaim?" But they said, "There has been no temple prostitute here."

22   So he returned to Judah, and said, "I did not find her; and furthermore, the men of the place said, 'There has been no temple prostitute here.'"

23   Then Judah said, "Let her keep them, otherwise we will become a laughingstock. After all, I sent this young goat, but you did not find her."

24   Now it was about three months later that Judah was informed, "Your daughter-in-law Tamar has played the harlot, and behold, she is also with child by harlotry." Then Judah said, "Bring her out and let her be burned!"

25   It was while she was being brought out that she sent to her father-in-law, saying, "I am with child by the man to whom these things belong." And she said, "Please examine and see, whose signet ring and cords and staff are these?"

26   Judah recognized them, and said, "She is more righteous than I, inasmuch as I did not give her to my son Shelah." And he did not have relations with her again.

27   It came about at the time she was giving birth, that behold, there were twins in her womb.

28   Moreover, it took place while she was giving birth, one put out a hand, and the midwife took and tied a scarlet thread on his hand, saying, "This one came out first."

29   But it came about as he drew back his hand, that behold, his brother came out. Then she said, "What a breach you have made for yourself!" So he was named Perez.

30   Afterward his brother came out who had the scarlet thread on his hand; and he was named Zerah.

Chapter 39

1   Now Joseph had been taken down to Egypt; and Potiphar, an Egyptian officer of Pharaoh, the captain of the bodyguard, bought him from the Ishmaelites, who had taken him down there.

2   The LORD was with Joseph, so he became a successful man. And he was in the house of his master, the Egyptian.

3   Now his master saw that the LORD was with him and how the LORD caused all that he did to prosper in his hand.

4   So Joseph found favor in his sight and became his personal servant; and he made him overseer over his house, and all that he owned he put in his charge.

5   It came about that from the time he made him overseer in his house and over all that he owned, the LORD blessed the Egyptian's house on account of Joseph; thus the LORD's blessing was upon all that he owned, in the house and in the field.

6   So he left everything he owned in Joseph's charge; and with him there he did not concern himself with anything except the food which he ate.
Now Joseph was handsome in form and appearance.

7   It came about after these events that his master's wife looked with desire at Joseph, and she said, "Lie with me."

8   But he refused and said to his master's wife, "Behold, with me here, my master does not concern himself with anything in the house, and he has put all that he owns in my charge.

9   "There is no one greater in this house than I, and he has withheld nothing from me except you, because you are his wife. How then could I do this great evil and sin against God?"

10   As she spoke to Joseph day after day, he did not listen to her to lie beside her or be with her.

11   Now it happened one day that he went into the house to do his work, and none of the men of the household was there inside.

12   She caught him by his garment, saying, "Lie with me!" And he left his garment in her hand and fled, and went outside.

13   When she saw that he had left his garment in her hand and had fled outside,

14   she called to the men of her household and said to them, "See, he has brought in a Hebrew to us to make sport of us; he came in to me to lie with me, and I screamed.

15   "When he heard that I raised my voice and screamed, he left his garment beside me and fled and went outside."

16   So she left his garment beside her until his master came home.

17   Then she spoke to him with these words, "The Hebrew slave, whom you brought to us, came in to me to make sport of me;

18   and as I raised my voice and screamed, he left his garment beside me and fled outside."

19   Now when his master heard the words of his wife, which she spoke to him, saying, "This is what your slave did to me," his anger burned.

20   So Joseph's master took him and put him into the jail, the place where the king's prisoners were confined; and he was there in the jail.

21   But the LORD was with Joseph and extended kindness to him, and gave him favor in the sight of the chief jailer.

22   The chief jailer committed to Joseph's charge all the prisoners who were in the jail; so that whatever was done there, he was responsible for it.

23   The chief jailer did not supervise anything under Joseph's charge because the LORD was with him; and whatever he did, the LORD made to prosper.

Chapter 40

1   Then it came about after these things, the cupbearer and the baker for the king of Egypt offended their lord, the king of Egypt.

2   Pharaoh was furious with his two officials, the chief cupbearer and the chief baker.

3   So he put them in confinement in the house of the captain of the bodyguard, in the jail, the same place where Joseph was imprisoned.

4   The captain of the bodyguard put Joseph in charge of them, and he took care of them; and they were in confinement for some time.

5   Then the cupbearer and the baker for the king of Egypt, who were confined in jail, both had a dream the same night, each man with his own dream and each dream with its own interpretation.

6   When Joseph came to them in the morning and observed them, behold, they were dejected.

7   He asked Pharaoh's officials who were with him in confinement in his master's house, "Why are your faces so sad today?"

8   Then they said to him, "We have had a dream and there is no one to interpret it." Then Joseph said to them, "Do not interpretations belong to God? Tell it to me, please."

9   So the chief cupbearer told his dream to Joseph, and said to him, "In my dream, behold, there was a vine in front of me;

10   and on the vine were three branches. And as it was budding, its blossoms came out, and its clusters produced ripe grapes.

11   "Now Pharaoh's cup was in my hand; so I took the grapes and squeezed them into Pharaoh's cup, and I put the cup into Pharaoh's hand."

12   Then Joseph said to him, "This is the interpretation of it: the three branches are three days;

13   within three more days Pharaoh will lift up your head and restore you to your office; and you will put Pharaoh's cup into his hand according to your former custom when you were his cupbearer.

14   "Only keep me in mind when it goes well with you, and please do me a kindness by mentioning me to Pharaoh and get me out of this house.

15   "For I was in fact kidnapped from the land of the Hebrews, and even here I have done nothing that they should have put me into the dungeon."

16   When the chief baker saw that he had interpreted favorably, he said to Joseph, "I also saw in my dream, and behold, there were three baskets of white bread on my head;

17   and in the top basket there were some of all sorts of baked food for Pharaoh, and the birds were eating them out of the basket on my head."

18   Then Joseph answered and said, "This is its interpretation: the three baskets are three days;

19   within three more days Pharaoh will lift up your head from you and will hang you on a tree, and the birds will eat your flesh off you."

20   Thus it came about on the third day, which was Pharaoh's birthday, that he made a feast for all his servants; and he lifted up the head of the chief cupbearer and the head of the chief baker among his servants.

21   He restored the chief cupbearer to his office, and he put the cup into Pharaoh's hand;

22   but he hanged the chief baker, just as Joseph had interpreted to them.

23   Yet the chief cupbearer did not remember Joseph, but forgot him.

Chapter 41

1   Now it happened at the end of two full years that Pharaoh had a dream, and behold, he was standing by the Nile.

2   And lo, from the Nile there came up seven cows, sleek and fat; and they grazed in the marsh grass.

3   Then behold, seven other cows came up after them from the Nile, ugly and gaunt, and they stood by the other cows on the bank of the Nile.

4   The ugly and gaunt cows ate up the seven sleek and fat cows. Then Pharaoh awoke.

5   He fell asleep and dreamed a second time; and behold, seven ears of grain came up on a single stalk, plump and good.

6   Then behold, seven ears, thin and scorched by the east wind, sprouted up after them.

7   The thin ears swallowed up the seven plump and full ears. Then Pharaoh awoke, and behold, it was a dream.

8   Now in the morning his spirit was troubled, so he sent and called for all the magicians of Egypt, and all its wise men. And Pharaoh told them his dreams, but there was no one who could interpret them to Pharaoh.

9   Then the chief cupbearer spoke to Pharaoh, saying, "I would make mention today of my own offenses.

10   "Pharaoh was furious with his servants, and he put me in confinement in the house of the captain of the bodyguard, both me and the chief baker.

11   "We had a dream on the same night, he and I; each of us dreamed according to the interpretation of his own dream.

12   "Now a Hebrew youth was with us there, a servant of the captain of the bodyguard, and we related them to him, and he interpreted our dreams for us. To each one he interpreted according to his own dream.

13   "And just as he interpreted for us, so it happened; he restored me in my office, but he hanged him."

14   Then Pharaoh sent and called for Joseph, and they hurriedly brought him out of the dungeon; and when he had shaved himself and changed his clothes, he came to Pharaoh.

15   Pharaoh said to Joseph, "I have had a dream, but no one can interpret it; and I have heard it said about you, that when you hear a dream you can interpret it."

16   Joseph then answered Pharaoh, saying, "It is not in me; God will give Pharaoh a favorable answer."

17   So Pharaoh spoke to Joseph, "In my dream, behold, I was standing on the bank of the Nile;

18 and behold, seven cows, fat and sleek came up out of the Nile, and they grazed in the marsh grass.

19 "Lo, seven other cows came up after them, poor and very ugly and gaunt, such as I had never seen for ugliness in all the land of Egypt;

20 and the lean and ugly cows ate up the first seven fat cows.

21 "Yet when they had devoured them, it could not be detected that they had devoured them, for they were just as ugly as before. Then I awoke.

22 "I saw also in my dream, and behold, seven ears, full and good, came up on a single stalk;

23 and lo, seven ears, withered, thin, and scorched by the east wind, sprouted up after them;

24 and the thin ears swallowed the seven good ears. Then I told it to the magicians, but there was no one who could explain it to me."

25 Now Joseph said to Pharaoh, "Pharaoh's dreams are one and the same; God has told to Pharaoh what He is about to do.

26 "The seven good cows are seven years; and the seven good ears are seven years; the dreams are one and the same.

27 "The seven lean and ugly cows that came up after them are seven years, and the seven thin ears scorched by the east wind will be seven years of famine.

28 "It is as I have spoken to Pharaoh: God has shown to Pharaoh what He is about to do.

29 "Behold, seven years of great abundance are coming in all the land of Egypt;

30 and after them seven years of famine will come, and all the abundance will be forgotten in the land of Egypt, and the famine will ravage the land.

31 "So the abundance will be unknown in the land because of that subsequent famine; for it will be very severe.

32   "Now as for the repeating of the dream to Pharaoh twice, it means that the matter is determined by God, and God will quickly bring it about.

33   "Now let Pharaoh look for a man discerning and wise, and set him over the land of Egypt.

34   "Let Pharaoh take action to appoint overseers in charge of the land, and let him exact a fifth of the produce of the land of Egypt in the seven years of abundance.

35   "Then let them gather all the food of these good years that are coming, and store up the grain for food in the cities under Pharaoh's authority, and let them guard it.

36   "Let the food become as a reserve for the land for the seven years of famine which will occur in the land of Egypt, so that the land will not perish during the famine."

37   Now the proposal seemed good to Pharaoh and to all his servants.

38   Then Pharaoh said to his servants, "Can we find a man like this, in whom is a divine spirit?"

39   So Pharaoh said to Joseph, "Since God has informed you of all this, there is no one so discerning and wise as you are.

40   "You shall be over my house, and according to your command all my people shall do homage; only in the throne I will be greater than you."

41   Pharaoh said to Joseph, "See, I have set you over all the land of Egypt."

42   Then Pharaoh took off his signet ring from his hand and put it on Joseph's hand, and clothed him in garments of fine linen and put the gold necklace around his neck.

43   He had him ride in his second chariot; and they proclaimed before him, "Bow the knee!" And he set him over all the land of Egypt.

44   Moreover, Pharaoh said to Joseph, "Though I am Pharaoh, yet without your permission no one shall raise his hand or foot in all the land of Egypt."

45 Then Pharaoh named Joseph Zaphenath-paneah; and he gave him Asenath, the daughter of Potiphera priest of On, as his wife. And Joseph went forth over the land of Egypt.

46 Now Joseph was thirty years old when he stood before Pharaoh, king of Egypt. And Joseph went out from the presence of Pharaoh and went through all the land of Egypt.

47 During the seven years of plenty the land brought forth abundantly.

48 So he gathered all the food of these seven years which occurred in the land of Egypt and placed the food in the cities; he placed in every city the food from its own surrounding fields.

49 Thus Joseph stored up grain in great abundance like the sand of the sea, until he stopped measuring it, for it was beyond measure.

50 Now before the year of famine came, two sons were born to Joseph, whom Asenath, the daughter of Potiphera priest of On, bore to him.

51 Joseph named the firstborn Manasseh, "For," he said, "God has made me forget all my trouble and all my father's household."

52 He named the second Ephraim, "For," he said, "God has made me fruitful in the land of my affliction."

53 When the seven years of plenty which had been in the land of Egypt came to an end,

54 and the seven years of famine began to come, just as Joseph had said, then there was famine in all the lands, but in all the land of Egypt there was bread.

55 So when all the land of Egypt was famished, the people cried out to Pharaoh for bread; and Pharaoh said to all the Egyptians, "Go to Joseph; whatever he says to you, you shall do."

56 When the famine was spread over all the face of the earth, then Joseph opened all the storehouses, and sold to the Egyptians; and the famine was severe in the land of Egypt.

57   The people of all the earth came to Egypt to buy grain from Joseph, because the famine was severe in all the earth.

Chapter 42

1   Now Jacob saw that there was grain in Egypt, and Jacob said to his sons, "Why are you staring at one another?"

2   He said, "Behold, I have heard that there is grain in Egypt; go down there and buy some for us from that place, so that we may live and not die."

3   Then ten brothers of Joseph went down to buy grain from Egypt.

4   But Jacob did not send Joseph's brother Benjamin with his brothers, for he said, "I am afraid that harm may befall him."

5   So the sons of Israel came to buy grain among those who were coming, for the famine was in the land of Canaan also.

6   Now Joseph was the ruler over the land; he was the one who sold to all the people of the land. And Joseph's brothers came and bowed down to him with their faces to the ground.

7   When Joseph saw his brothers he recognized them, but he disguised himself to them and spoke to them harshly. And he said to them, "Where have you come from?" And they said, "From the land of Canaan, to buy food."

8   But Joseph had recognized his brothers, although they did not recognize him.

9   Joseph remembered the dreams which he had about them, and said to them, "You are spies; you have come to look at the undefended parts of our land."

10   Then they said to him, "No, my lord, but your servants have come to buy food.

11   "We are all sons of one man; we are honest men, your servants are not spies."

12   Yet he said to them, "No, but you have come to look at the undefended parts of our land!"

13   But they said, "Your servants are twelve brothers in all, the sons of one man in the land of Canaan; and behold, the youngest is with our father today, and one is no longer alive."

14   Joseph said to them, "It is as I said to you, you are spies;

15   by this you will be tested: by the life of Pharaoh, you shall not go from this place unless your youngest brother comes here!

16   "Send one of you that he may get your brother, while you remain confined, that your words may be tested, whether there is truth in you. But if not, by the life of Pharaoh, surely you are spies."

17   So he put them all together in prison for three days.

18   Now Joseph said to them on the third day, "Do this and live, for I fear God:

19   if you are honest men, let one of your brothers be confined in your prison; but as for the rest of you, go, carry grain for the famine of your households,

20   and bring your youngest brother to me, so your words may be verified, and you will not die." And they did so.

21   Then they said to one another, "Truly we are guilty concerning our brother, because we saw the distress of his soul when he pleaded with us, yet we would not listen; therefore this distress has come upon us."

22   Reuben answered them, saying, "Did I not tell you, 'Do not sin against the boy; and you would not listen? Now comes the reckoning for his blood."

23   They did not know, however, that Joseph understood, for there was an interpreter between them.

24   He turned away from them and wept. But when he returned to them and spoke to them, he took Simeon from them and bound him before their eyes.

25   Then Joseph gave orders to fill their bags with grain and to restore every man's money in his sack, and to give them provisions for the journey. And thus it was done for them.

26   So they loaded their donkeys with their grain and departed from there.

27   As one of them opened his sack to give his donkey fodder at the lodging place, he saw his money; and behold, it was in the mouth of his sack.

28   Then he said to his brothers, "My money has been returned, and behold, it is even in my sack." And their hearts sank, and they turned trembling to one another, saying, "What is this that God has done to us?"

29   When they came to their father Jacob in the land of Canaan, they told him all that had happened to them, saying,

30   "The man, the lord of the land, spoke harshly with us, and took us for spies of the country.

31   "But we said to him, 'We are honest men; we are not spies.

32   We are twelve brothers, sons of our father; one is no longer alive, and the youngest is with our father today in the land of Canaan.'

33   "The man, the lord of the land, said to us, 'By this I will know that you are honest men: leave one of your brothers with me and take grain for the famine of your households, and go.

34   'But bring your youngest brother to me that I may know that you are not spies, but honest men. I will give your brother to you, and you may trade in the land.'"

35   Now it came about as they were emptying their sacks, that behold, every man's bundle of money was in his sack; and when they and their father saw their bundles of money, they were dismayed.

36   Their father Jacob said to them, "You have bereaved me of my children: Joseph is no more, and Simeon is no more, and you would take Benjamin; all these things are against me."

37   Then Reuben spoke to his father, saying, "You may put my two sons to death if I do not bring him back to you; put him in my care, and I will return him to you."

38   But Jacob said, "My son shall not go down with you; for his brother is dead, and he alone is left. If harm should befall him on the journey you are taking, then you will bring my gray hair down to Sheol in sorrow."

Chapter 43

1   Now the famine was severe in the land.

2   So it came about when they had finished eating the grain which they had brought from Egypt, that their father said to them, "Go back, buy us a little food."

3   Judah spoke to him, however, saying, "The man solemnly warned us, 'You shall not see my face unless your brother is with you.'

4   "If you send our brother with us, we will go down and buy you food.

5   "But if you do not send him, we will not go down; for the man said to us, 'You will not see my face unless your brother is with you.'"

6   Then Israel said, "Why did you treat me so badly by telling the man whether you still had another brother?"

7   But they said, "The man questioned particularly about us and our relatives, saying, 'Is your father still alive? Have you another brother?' So we answered his questions. Could we possibly know that he would say, 'Bring your brother down'?"

8   Judah said to his father Israel, "Send the lad with me and we will arise and go, that we may live and not die, we as well as you and our little ones.

9   "I myself will be surety for him; you may hold me responsible for him. If I do not bring him back to you and set him before you, then let me bear the blame before you forever.

10   "For if we had not delayed, surely by now we could have returned twice."

11   Then their father Israel said to them, "If it must be so, then do this: take some of the best products of the land in your bags, and carry down to the man as a present, a little balm and a little honey, aromatic gum and myrrh, pistachio nuts and almonds.

12   "Take double the money in your hand, and take back in your hand the money that was returned in the mouth of your sacks; perhaps it was a mistake.

13   "Take your brother also, and arise, return to the man;

14   and may God Almighty grant you compassion in the sight of the man, so that he will release to you your other brother and Benjamin. And as for me, if I am bereaved of my children, I am bereaved."

15   So the men took this present, and they took double the money in their hand, and Benjamin; then they arose and went down to Egypt and stood before Joseph.

16   When Joseph saw Benjamin with them, he said to his house steward, "Bring the men into the house, and slay an animal and make ready; for the men are to dine with me at noon."

17   So the man did as Joseph said, and brought the men to Joseph's house.

18   Now the men were afraid, because they were brought to Joseph's house; and they said, "It is because of the money that was returned in our sacks the first time that we are being brought in, that he may seek occasion against us and fall upon us, and take us for slaves with our donkeys."

19   So they came near to Joseph's house steward, and spoke to him at the entrance of the house,

20   and said, "Oh, my lord, we indeed came down the first time to buy food,

21   and it came about when we came to the lodging place, that we opened our sacks, and behold, each man's money was in the mouth of his sack, our money in full. So we have brought it back in our hand.

22   "We have also brought down other money in our hand to buy food; we do not know who put our money in our sacks."

23   He said, "Be at ease, do not be afraid. Your God and the God of your father has given you treasure in your sacks; I had your money." Then he brought Simeon out to them.

24   Then the man brought the men into Joseph's house and gave them water, and they washed their feet; and he gave their donkeys fodder.

25   So they prepared the present for Joseph's coming at noon; for they had heard that they were to eat a meal there.

26   When Joseph came home, they brought into the house to him the present which was in their hand and bowed to the ground before him.

27   Then he asked them about their welfare, and said, "Is your old father well, of whom you spoke? Is he still alive?"

28   They said, "Your servant our father is well; he is still alive." They bowed down in homage.

29   As he lifted his eyes and saw his brother Benjamin, his mother's son, he said, "Is this your youngest brother, of whom you spoke to me?" And he said, "May God be gracious to you, my son."

30   Joseph hurried out for he was deeply stirred over his brother, and he sought a place to weep; and he entered his chamber and wept there.

31   Then he washed his face and came out; and he controlled himself and said, "Serve the meal."

32　So they served him by himself, and them by themselves, and the Egyptians who ate with him by themselves, because the Egyptians could not eat bread with the Hebrews, for that is loathsome to the Egyptians.

33　Now they were seated before him, the firstborn according to his birthright and the youngest according to his youth, and the men looked at one another in astonishment.

34　He took portions to them from his own table, but Benjamin's portion was five times as much as any of theirs. So they feasted and drank freely with him.

Chapter 44

1　Then he commanded his house steward, saying, "Fill the men's sacks with food, as much as they can carry, and put each man's money in the mouth of his sack.

2　"Put my cup, the silver cup, in the mouth of the sack of the youngest, and his money for the grain." And he did as Joseph had told him.

3　As soon as it was light, the men were sent away, they with their donkeys.

4　They had just gone out of the city, and were not far off, when Joseph said to his house steward, "Up, follow the men; and when you overtake them, say to them, 'Why have you repaid evil for good?

5　'Is not this the one from which my lord drinks and which he indeed uses for divination? You have done wrong in doing this.'"

6　So he overtook them and spoke these words to them.

7　They said to him, "Why does my lord speak such words as these? Far be it from your servants to do such a thing.

8　"Behold, the money which we found in the mouth of our sacks we have brought back to you from the land of Canaan. How then could we steal silver or gold from your lord's house?

9   "With whomever of your servants it is found, let him die, and we also will be my lord's slaves."

10   So he said, "Now let it also be according to your words; he with whom it is found shall be my slave, and the rest of you shall be innocent."

11   Then they hurried, each man lowered his sack to the ground, and each man opened his sack.

12   He searched, beginning with the oldest and ending with the youngest, and the cup was found in Benjamin's sack.

13   Then they tore their clothes, and when each man loaded his donkey, they returned to the city.

14   When Judah and his brothers came to Joseph's house, he was still there, and they fell to the ground before him.

15   Joseph said to them, "What is this deed that you have done? Do you not know that such a man as I can indeed practice divination?"

16   So Judah said, "What can we say to my lord? What can we speak? And how can we justify ourselves? God has found out the iniquity of your servants; behold, we are my lord's slaves, both we and the one in whose possession the cup has been found."

17   But he said, "Far be it from me to do this. The man in whose possession the cup has been found, he shall be my slave; but as for you, go up in peace to your father."

18   Then Judah approached him, and said, "Oh my lord, may your servant please speak a word in my lord's ears, and do not be angry with your servant; for you are equal to Pharaoh.

19   "My lord asked his servants, saying, 'Have you a father or a brother?'

20   "We said to my lord, 'We have an old father and a little child of his old age. Now his brother is dead, so he alone is left of his mother, and his father loves him.'

21   "Then you said to your servants, 'Bring him down to me that I may set my eyes on him.'

22   "But we said to my lord, 'The lad cannot leave his father, for if he should leave his father, his father would die.'

23   "You said to your servants, however, 'Unless your youngest brother comes down with you, you will not see my face again.'

24   "Thus it came about when we went up to your servant my father, we told him the words of my lord.

25   "Our father said, 'Go back, buy us a little food.'

26   "But we said, 'We cannot go down. If our youngest brother is with us, then we will go down; for we cannot see the man's face unless our youngest brother is with us.'

27   "Your servant my father said to us, 'You know that my wife bore me two sons;

28   and the one went out from me, and I said, "Surely he is torn in pieces," and I have not seen him since.

29   If you take this one also from me, and harm befalls him, you will bring my gray hair down to Sheol in sorrow.'

30   "Now, therefore, when I come to your servant my father, and the lad is not with us, since his life is bound up in the lad's life,

31   when he sees that the lad is not with us, he will die. Thus your servants will bring the gray hair of your servant our father down to Sheol in sorrow.

32   "For your servant became surety for the lad to my father, saying, 'If I do not bring him back to you, then let me bear the blame before my father forever.'

33   "Now, therefore, please let your servant remain instead of the lad a slave to my lord, and let the lad go up with his brothers.

34   "For how shall I go up to my father if the lad is not with me—for fear that I see the evil that would overtake my father?"

Chapter 45

1 Then Joseph could not control himself before all those who stood by him, and he cried, "Have everyone go out from me." So there was no man with him when Joseph made himself known to his brothers.

2 He wept so loudly that the Egyptians heard it, and the household of Pharaoh heard of it.

3 Then Joseph said to his brothers, "I am Joseph! Is my father still alive?" But his brothers could not answer him, for they were dismayed at his presence.

4 Then Joseph said to his brothers, "Please come closer to me." And they came closer. And he said, "I am your brother Joseph, whom you sold into Egypt.

5 "Now do not be grieved or angry with yourselves, because you sold me here, for God sent me before you to preserve life.

6 "For the famine has been in the land these two years, and there are still five years in which there will be neither plowing nor harvesting.

7 "God sent me before you to preserve for you a remnant in the earth, and to keep you alive by a great deliverance.

8 "Now, therefore, it was not you who sent me here, but God; and He has made me a father to Pharaoh and lord of all his household and ruler over all the land of Egypt.

9 "Hurry and go up to my father, and say to him, 'Thus says your son Joseph, "God has made me lord of all Egypt; come down to me, do not delay.

10 "You shall live in the land of Goshen, and you shall be near me, you and your children and your children's children and your flocks and your herds and all that you have.

11 "There I will also provide for you, for there are still five years of famine to come, and you and your household and all that you have would be impoverished."'

12   "Behold, your eyes see, and the eyes of my brother Benjamin see, that it is my mouth which is speaking to you.

13   "Now you must tell my father of all my splendor in Egypt, and all that you have seen; and you must hurry and bring my father down here."

14   Then he fell on his brother Benjamin's neck and wept, and Benjamin wept on his neck.

15   He kissed all his brothers and wept on them, and afterward his brothers talked with him.

16   Now when the news was heard in Pharaoh's house that Joseph's brothers had come, it pleased Pharaoh and his servants.

17   Then Pharaoh said to Joseph, "Say to your brothers, 'Do this: load your beasts and go to the land of Canaan,

18   and take your father and your households and come to me, and I will give you the best of the land of Egypt and you will eat the fat of the land.'

19   "Now you are ordered, 'Do this: take wagons from the land of Egypt for your little ones and for your wives, and bring your father and come.

20   'Do not concern yourselves with your goods, for the best of all the land of Egypt is yours.'"

21   Then the sons of Israel did so; and Joseph gave them wagons according to the command of Pharaoh, and gave them provisions for the journey.

22   To each of them he gave changes of garments, but to Benjamin he gave three hundred pieces of silver and five changes of garments.

23   To his father he sent as follows: ten donkeys loaded with the best things of Egypt, and ten female donkeys loaded with grain and bread and sustenance for his father on the journey.

24   So he sent his brothers away, and as they departed, he said to them, "Do not quarrel on the journey."

25   Then they went up from Egypt, and came to the land of Canaan to their father Jacob.

26   They told him, saying, "Joseph is still alive, and indeed he is ruler over all the land of Egypt." But he was stunned, for he did not believe them.

27   When they told him all the words of Joseph that he had spoken to them, and when he saw the wagons that Joseph had sent to carry him, the spirit of their father Jacob revived.

28   Then Israel said, "It is enough; my son Joseph is still alive. I will go and see him before I die."

Chapter 46

1   So Israel set out with all that he had, and came to Beersheba, and offered sacrifices to the God of his father Isaac.

2   God spoke to Israel in visions of the night and said, "Jacob, Jacob." And he said, "Here I am."

3   He said, "I am God, the God of your father; do not be afraid to go down to Egypt, for I will make you a great nation there.

4   "I will go down with you to Egypt, and I will also surely bring you up again; and Joseph will close your eyes."

5   Then Jacob arose from Beersheba; and the sons of Israel carried their father Jacob and their little ones and their wives in the wagons which Pharaoh had sent to carry him.

6   They took their livestock and their property, which they had acquired in the land of Canaan, and came to Egypt, Jacob and all his descendants with him:

7   his sons and his grandsons with him, his daughters and his granddaughters, and all his descendants he brought with him to Egypt.

8   Now these are the names of the sons of Israel, Jacob and his sons, who went to Egypt: Reuben, Jacob's firstborn.

9　The sons of Reuben: Hanoch and Pallu and Hezron and Carmi.

10　The sons of Simeon: Jemuel and Jamin and Ohad and Jachin and Zohar and Shaul the son of a Canaanite woman.

11　The sons of Levi: Gershon, Kohath, and Merari.

12　The sons of Judah: Er and Onan and Shelah and Perez and Zerah (but Er and Onan died in the land of Canaan). And the sons of Perez were Hezron and Hamul.

13　The sons of Issachar: Tola and Puvvah and Iob and Shimron.

14　The sons of Zebulun: Sered and Elon and Jahleel.

15　These are the sons of Leah, whom she bore to Jacob in Paddan-aram, with his daughter Dinah; all his sons and his daughters numbered thirty-three.

16　The sons of Gad: Ziphion and Haggi, Shuni and Ezbon, Eri and Arodi and Areli.

17　The sons of Asher: Imnah and Ishvah and Ishvi and Beriah and their sister Serah. And the sons of Beriah: Heber and Malchiel.

18　These are the sons of Zilpah, whom Laban gave to his daughter Leah; and she bore to Jacob these sixteen persons.

19　The sons of Jacob's wife Rachel: Joseph and Benjamin.

20　Now to Joseph in the land of Egypt were born Manasseh and Ephraim, whom Asenath, the daughter of Potiphera, priest of On, bore to him.

21　The sons of Benjamin: Bela and Becher and Ashbel, Gera and Naaman, Ehi and Rosh, Muppim and Huppim and Ard.

22　These are the sons of Rachel, who were born to Jacob; there were fourteen persons in all.

23　The sons of Dan: Hushim.

24　The sons of Naphtali: Jahzeel and Guni and Jezer and Shillem.

25　These are the sons of Bilhah, whom Laban gave to his daughter Rachel, and she bore these to Jacob; there were seven persons in all.

26   All the persons belonging to Jacob, who came to Egypt, his direct descendants, not including the wives of Jacob's sons, were sixty-six persons in all,

27   and the sons of Joseph, who were born to him in Egypt were two; all the persons of the house of Jacob, who came to Egypt, were seventy.

28   Now he sent Judah before him to Joseph, to point out the way before him to Goshen; and they came into the land of Goshen.

29   Joseph prepared his chariot and went up to Goshen to meet his father Israel; as soon as he appeared before him, he fell on his neck and wept on his neck a long time.

30   Then Israel said to Joseph, "Now let me die, since I have seen your face, that you are still alive."

31   Joseph said to his brothers and to his father's household, "I will go up and tell Pharaoh, and will say to him, 'My brothers and my father's household, who were in the land of Canaan, have come to me;

32   and the men are shepherds, for they have been keepers of livestock; and they have brought their flocks and their herds and all that they have.'

33   "When Pharaoh calls you and says, 'What is your occupation?'

34   you shall say, 'Your servants have been keepers of livestock from our youth even until now, both we and our fathers,' that you may live in the land of Goshen; for every shepherd is loathsome to the Egyptians."

Chapter 47

1   Then Joseph went in and told Pharaoh, and said, "My father and my brothers and their flocks and their herds and all that they have, have come out of the land of Canaan; and behold, they are in the land of Goshen."

2   He took five men from among his brothers and presented them to Pharaoh.

3   Then Pharaoh said to his brothers, "What is your occupation?" So they said to Pharaoh, "Your servants are shepherds, both we and our fathers."

4   They said to Pharaoh, "We have come to sojourn in the land, for there is no pasture for your servants' flocks, for the famine is severe in the land of Canaan. Now, therefore, please let your servants live in the land of Goshen."

5   Then Pharaoh said to Joseph, "Your father and your brothers have come to you.

6   "The land of Egypt is at your disposal; settle your father and your brothers in the best of the land, let them live in the land of Goshen; and if you know any capable men among them, then put them in charge of my livestock."

7   Then Joseph brought his father Jacob and presented him to Pharaoh; and Jacob blessed Pharaoh.

8   Pharaoh said to Jacob, "How many years have you lived?"

9   So Jacob said to Pharaoh, "The years of my sojourning are one hundred and thirty; few and unpleasant have been the years of my life, nor have they attained the years that my fathers lived during the days of their sojourning."

10   And Jacob blessed Pharaoh, and went out from his presence.

11   So Joseph settled his father and his brothers and gave them a possession in the land of Egypt, in the best of the land, in the land of Rameses, as Pharaoh had ordered.

12   Joseph provided his father and his brothers and all his father's household with food, according to their little ones.

13   Now there was no food in all the land, because the famine was very severe, so that the land of Egypt and the land of Canaan languished because of the famine.

14   Joseph gathered all the money that was found in the land of Egypt and in the land of Canaan for the grain which they bought, and Joseph brought the money into Pharaoh's house.

15   When the money was all spent in the land of Egypt and in the land of Canaan, all the Egyptians came to Joseph and said, "Give us food, for why should we die in your presence? For our money is gone."

16   Then Joseph said, "Give up your livestock, and I will give you food for your livestock, since your money is gone."

17   So they brought their livestock to Joseph, and Joseph gave them food in exchange for the horses and the flocks and the herds and the donkeys; and he fed them with food in exchange for all their livestock that year.

18   When that year was ended, they came to him the next year and said to him, "We will not hide from my lord that our money is all spent, and the cattle are my lord's. There is nothing left for my lord except our bodies and our lands.

19   "Why should we die before your eyes, both we and our land? Buy us and our land for food, and we and our land will be slaves to Pharaoh. So give us seed, that we may live and not die, and that the land may not be desolate."

20   So Joseph bought all the land of Egypt for Pharaoh, for every Egyptian sold his field, because the famine was severe upon them. Thus the land became Pharaoh's.

21   As for the people, he removed them to the cities from one end of Egypt's border to the other.

22   Only the land of the priests he did not buy, for the priests had an allotment from Pharaoh, and they lived off the allotment which Pharaoh gave them. Therefore, they did not sell their land.

23   Then Joseph said to the people, "Behold, I have today bought you and your land for Pharaoh; now, here is seed for you, and you may sow the land.

24   "At the harvest you shall give a fifth to Pharaoh, and four-fifths shall be your own for seed of the field and for your food and for those of your households and as food for your little ones."

25   So they said, "You have saved our lives! Let us find favor in the sight of my lord, and we will be Pharaoh's slaves."

26   Joseph made it a statute concerning the land of Egypt valid to this day, that Pharaoh should have the fifth; only the land of the priests did not become Pharaoh's.

27   Now Israel lived in the land of Egypt, in Goshen, and they acquired property in it and were fruitful and became very numerous.

28   Jacob lived in the land of Egypt seventeen years; so the length of Jacob's life was one hundred and forty-seven years.

29   When the time for Israel to die drew near, he called his son Joseph and said to him, "Please, if I have found favor in your sight, place now your hand under my thigh and deal with me in kindness and faithfulness. Please do not bury me in Egypt,

30   but when I lie down with my fathers, you shall carry me out of Egypt and bury me in their burial place." And he said, "I will do as you have said."

31   He said, "Swear to me." So he swore to him. Then Israel bowed in worship at the head of the bed.

Chapter 48

1   Now it came about after these things that Joseph was told, "Behold, your father is sick." So he took his two sons Manasseh and Ephraim with him.

2   When it was told to Jacob, "Behold, your son Joseph has come to you," Israel collected his strength and sat up in the bed.

3   Then Jacob said to Joseph, "God Almighty appeared to me at Luz in the land of Canaan and blessed me,

4   and He said to me, 'Behold, I will make you fruitful and numerous, and I will make you a company of peoples, and will give this land to your descendants after you for an everlasting possession.'

5   "Now your two sons, who were born to you in the land of Egypt before I came to you in Egypt, are mine; Ephraim and Manasseh shall be mine, as Reuben and Simeon are.

6   "But your offspring that have been born after them shall be yours; they shall be called by the names of their brothers in their inheritance.

7   "Now as for me, when I came from Paddan, Rachel died, to my sorrow, in the land of Canaan on the journey, when there was still some distance to go to Ephrath; and I buried her there on the way to Ephrath (that is, Bethlehem)."

8   When Israel saw Joseph's sons, he said, "Who are these?"

9   Joseph said to his father, "They are my sons, whom God has given me here." So he said, "Bring them to me, please, that I may bless them."

10   Now the eyes of Israel were so dim from age that he could not see. Then Joseph brought them close to him, and he kissed them and embraced them.

11   Israel said to Joseph, "I never expected to see your face, and behold, God has let me see your children as well."

12   Then Joseph took them from his knees, and bowed with his face to the ground.

13   Joseph took them both, Ephraim with his right hand toward Israel's left, and Manasseh with his left hand toward Israel's right, and brought them close to him.

14   But Israel stretched out his right hand and laid it on the head of Ephraim, who was the younger, and his left hand on Manasseh's head, crossing his hands, although Manasseh was the firstborn.

15   He blessed Joseph, and said,

> "The God before whom my fathers Abraham and
> Isaac walked,
> The God who has been my shepherd all my life to this day,

16   The angel who has redeemed me from all evil,

> Bless the lads;
> And may my name live on in them,
> And the names of my fathers Abraham and Isaac;
> And may they grow into a multitude in the midst of
> the earth."

17   When Joseph saw that his father laid his right hand on Ephraim's head, it displeased him; and he grasped his father's hand to remove it from Ephraim's head to Manasseh's head.

18   Joseph said to his father, "Not so, my father, for this one is the firstborn. Place your right hand on his head."

19   But his father refused and said, "I know, my son, I know; he also will become a people and he also will be great. However, his younger brother shall be greater than he, and his descendants shall become a multitude of nations."

20   He blessed them that day, saying,

> "By you Israel will pronounce blessing, saying,
> 'May God make you like Ephraim and Manasseh!'"

Thus he put Ephraim before Manasseh.

21   Then Israel said to Joseph, "Behold, I am about to die, but God will be with you, and bring you back to the land of your fathers.

22   "I give you one portion more than your brothers, which I took from the hand of the Amorite with my sword and my bow."

Chapter 49

1   Then Jacob summoned his sons and said, "Assemble yourselves that
I may tell you what will befall you in the days to come.

2   "Gather together and hear, O sons of Jacob;

    And listen to Israel your father.

3   "Reuben, you are my firstborn;

    My might and the beginning of my strength,

    Preeminent in dignity and preeminent in power.

4   "Uncontrolled as water, you shall not have preeminence,

    Because you went up to your father's bed;

    Then you defiled it—he went up to my couch.

5   "Simeon and Levi are brothers;

    Their swords are implements of violence.

6   "Let my soul not enter into their council;

    Let not my glory be united with their assembly;

    Because in their anger they slew men,

    And in their self-will they lamed oxen.

7   "Cursed be their anger, for it is fierce;

    And their wrath, for it is cruel.

    I will disperse them in Jacob,

    And scatter them in Israel.

8   "Judah, your brothers shall praise you;

    Your hand shall be on the neck of your enemies;

    Your father's sons shall bow down to you.

9   "Judah is a lion's whelp;

    From the prey, my son, you have gone up.

    He couches, he lies down as a lion,

    And as a lion, who dares rouse him up?

10   "The scepter shall not depart from Judah,

      Nor the ruler's staff from between his feet,

      Until Shiloh comes,

      And to him shall be the obedience of the peoples.

11   "He ties his foal to the vine,

      And his donkey's colt to the choice vine;

      He washes his garments in wine,

      And his robes in the blood of grapes.

12   "His eyes are dull from wine,

      And his teeth white from milk.

13   "Zebulun will dwell at the seashore;

      And he shall be a haven for ships,

      And his flank shall be toward Sidon.

14   "Issachar is a strong donkey,

      Lying down between the sheepfolds.

15   "When he saw that a resting place was good

      And that the land was pleasant,

      He bowed his shoulder to bear burdens,

      And became a slave at forced labor.

16   "Dan shall judge his people,

      As one of the tribes of Israel.

17   "Dan shall be a serpent in the way,

      A horned snake in the path,

      That bites the horse's heels,

      So that his rider falls backward.

18   "For Your salvation I wait, O LORD.

19   "As for Gad, raiders shall raid him,

      But he will raid at their heels.

20   "As for Asher, his food shall be rich,

And he will yield royal dainties.

21   "Naphtali is a doe let loose,

He gives beautiful words.

22   "Joseph is a fruitful bough,

A fruitful bough by a spring;

Its branches run over a wall.

23   "The archers bitterly attacked him,

And shot at him and harassed him;

24   But his bow remained firm,

And his arms were agile,

From the hands of the Mighty One of Jacob

(From there is the Shepherd, the Stone of Israel),

25   From the God of your father who helps you,

And by the Almighty who blesses you

With blessings of heaven above,

Blessings of the deep that lies beneath,

Blessings of the breasts and of the womb.

26   "The blessings of your father

Have surpassed the blessings of my ancestors

Up to the utmost bound of the everlasting hills;

May they be on the head of Joseph,

And on the crown of the head of the one distinguished among his

brothers.

27   "Benjamin is a ravenous wolf;

In the morning he devours the prey,

And in the evening he divides the spoil."

28   All these are the twelve tribes of Israel, and this is what their father
said to them when he blessed them. He blessed them, every one with the
blessing appropriate to him.

29   Then he charged them and said to them, "I am about to be gathered to my people; bury me with my fathers in the cave that is in the field of Ephron the Hittite,

30   in the cave that is in the field of Machpelah, which is before Mamre, in the land of Canaan, which Abraham bought along with the field from Ephron the Hittite for a burial site.

31   "There they buried Abraham and his wife Sarah, there they buried Isaac and his wife Rebekah, and there I buried Leah—

32   the field and the cave that is in it, purchased from the sons of Heth."

33   When Jacob finished charging his sons, he drew his feet into the bed and breathed his last, and was gathered to his people.

Chapter 50

1   Then Joseph fell on his father's face, and wept over him and kissed him.

2   Joseph commanded his servants the physicians to embalm his father. So the physicians embalmed Israel.

3   Now forty days were required for it, for such is the period required for embalming. And the Egyptians wept for him seventy days.

4   When the days of mourning for him were past, Joseph spoke to the household of Pharaoh, saying, "If now I have found favor in your sight, please speak to Pharaoh, saying,

5   'My father made me swear, saying, "Behold, I am about to die; in my grave which I dug for myself in the land of Canaan, there you shall bury me." Now therefore, please let me go up and bury my father; then I will return.'"

6   Pharaoh said, "Go up and bury your father, as he made you swear."

7   So Joseph went up to bury his father, and with him went up all the servants of Pharaoh, the elders of his household and all the elders of the land of Egypt,

8   and all the household of Joseph and his brothers and his father's household; they left only their little ones and their flocks and their herds in the land of Goshen.

9   There also went up with him both chariots and horsemen; and it was a very great company.

10   When they came to the threshing floor of Atad, which is beyond the Jordan, they lamented there with a very great and sorrowful lamentation; and he observed seven days mourning for his father.

11   Now when the inhabitants of the land, the Canaanites, saw the mourning at the threshing floor of Atad, they said, "This is a grievous mourning for the Egyptians." Therefore it was named Abel-mizraim, which is beyond the Jordan.

12   Thus his sons did for him as he had charged them;

13   for his sons carried him to the land of Canaan and buried him in the cave of the field of Machpelah before Mamre, which Abraham had bought along with the field for a burial site from Ephron the Hittite.

14   After he had buried his father, Joseph returned to Egypt, he and his brothers, and all who had gone up with him to bury his father.

15   When Joseph's brothers saw that their father was dead, they said, "What if Joseph bears a grudge against us and pays us back in full for all the wrong which we did to him!"

16   So they sent a message to Joseph, saying, "Your father charged before he died, saying,

17   'Thus you shall say to Joseph, "Please forgive, I beg you, the transgression of your brothers and their sin, for they did you wrong."' And now, please forgive the transgression of the servants of the God of your father." And Joseph wept when they spoke to him.

18   Then his brothers also came and fell down before him and said, "Behold, we are your servants."

19   But Joseph said to them, "Do not be afraid, for am I in God's place?

20   "As for you, you meant evil against me, but God meant it for good in order to bring about this present result, to preserve many people alive.

21   "So therefore, do not be afraid; I will provide for you and your little ones." So he comforted them and spoke kindly to them.

22   Now Joseph stayed in Egypt, he and his father's household, and Joseph lived one hundred and ten years.

23   Joseph saw the third generation of Ephraim's sons; also the sons of Machir, the son of Manasseh, were born on Joseph's knees.

24   Joseph said to his brothers, "I am about to die, but God will surely take care of you and bring you up from this land to the land which He promised on oath to Abraham, to Isaac and to Jacob."

25   Then Joseph made the sons of Israel swear, saying, "God will surely take care of you, and you shall carry my bones up from here."

26   So Joseph died at the age of one hundred and ten years; and he was embalmed and placed in a coffin in Egypt.

DiSCOVER 4 YOURSELF!

iNDUCTiVE BiBLE STUDiES FOR KiDS

Bible study can be fun! Now kids can learn how to inductively study the Bible to discover for themselves what it says. Each book combines serious Bible study with memorable games, puzzles, and activities that reinforce biblical truth. Divided into short lessons, each individual study includes:

- a weekly memory verse
- Bible knowledge activities—puzzles, games, and discovery activities
- Optional crafts and projects to help kids practice what they've learned

Any young person who works through these studies will emerge with a richer appreciation for the Word of God and a deeper understanding of God's love and care.

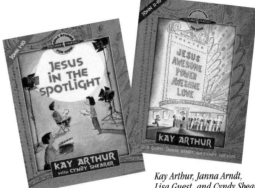

Kay Arthur and Cyndy Shearer
Kids "make" a movie to discover who Jesus is and His impact on their lives. Activities and 15-minute lessons make this study of John 1–10 great for all ages!
ISBN 0-7369-0119-1

Kay Arthur, Janna Arndt, Lisa Guest, and Cyndy Shearer
This book picks up where *Jesus in the Spotlight* leaves off: John 11–16. Kids join a movie team to bring the life of Jesus to the big screen in order to learn key truths about prayer, heaven, and Jesus.
ISBN 0-7369-0144-2

Kay Arthur and Janna Arndt
As "advice columnists," kids delve into the book of James to discover—and learn how to apply—the best answers for a variety of problems.
ISBN 0-7369-0148-5

Kay Arthur and Janna Arndt
This easy-to-use Bible study combines serious commitment to God's Word with illustrations and activities that reinforce biblical truth.
ISBN 0-7369-0362-3

Kay Arthur and Janna Arndt
Focusing on John 17–21, children become "directors" who must discover the details of Jesus' life to make a great movie. They also learn how to get the most out of reading their Bibles.
ISBN 0-7369-0546-4

Kay Arthur and Scoti Domeij
As "reporters," kids investigate Jonah's story and conduct interviews. Using puzzles and activities, these lessons highlight God's loving care and the importance of obedience.
ISBN 0-7369-0203-1

Kay Arthur and Janna Arndt
God's Amazing Creation covers Genesis 1–2-those awesome days when God created the stars, the world, the sea, the animals, and the very first people. Young explorers will go on an archaeological dig to discover truths for themselves!
ISBN 0-7369-0143-4

Kay Arthur and Janna Arndt
Kids become archaeologists to uncover how God deals with sin, where different languages and nations came from, and what God's plan is for saving people (Genesis 3–11).
ISBN 0-7369-0374-7

Everybody, Everywhere, Anytime, Anyplace, Any Age...
Can Discover the Truth for Themselves

In today's world with its often confusing and mixed messages, where can you turn to find the answer to the challenges you and your family face? Whose word can you trust? Where can you turn when you need answers—about relationships, your children, your future?

The Updated New Inductive Study Bible

Open *this* study Bible and you will soon discover its uniqueness—unlike any other, this study Bible offers no notes, commentaries, or the opinions of others telling you what the Scripture is saying. It is in fact the only study Bible based entirely on the *inductive* study approach, providing you with instructions and the tools for observing what the text really says, interpreting what it means, and applying its principles to your life.

The only study Bible containing the *inductive study method* taught and endorsed by Kay Arthur and Precept Ministries.

• A new *smaller* size makes it easier to carry • individualized instructions for studying *every* book • guides for color marking keywords and themes • *Updated* NASB text • *improved* in-text maps and charts • 24 pages of full-color charts, historical timelines, & maps • self-discovery in its truest form

One Message, The Bible.

A SIMPLE, PROVEN APPROACH TO LETTING GOD'S WORD CHANGE YOUR LIFE...FOREVER

One Method, Inductive.

Experience the inductive study method—for a free excerpt call:
1-800-763-8280
or visit www.inductivestudy.com

Available at bookstores everywhere

HARVEST HOUSE PUBLISHERS
EUGENE, OREGON 97402